EDITOR: Maryanne Blacker

DESIGN DIRECTOR: Neil Carlyle

■ ■ ■

ASSISTANT EDITOR: Judy Newman

DESIGNERS: Louise McGeachie, Robbylee Phelan

SUB-EDITORS: Mary-Anne Danaher, Danielle Farah

SECRETARY: Wendy Moore

■ ■ ■

PHOTOGRAPHER: Rodney Weidland

■ ■ ■

ILLUSTRATIONS: Sue Ninham

■ ■ ■

SEWING: Betty Smith, Jenny Manning,
Diana Buttigieg, Yvette Abboud

■ ■ ■

PUBLISHER: Richard Walsh

DEPUTY PUBLISHER: Graham Lawrence

■ ■ ■

Produced by The Australian Women's Weekly
Home Library
Typeset by Letter Perfect, Sydney.
Printed by Dai Nippon Co Ltd, Tokyo, Japan
Published by Australian Consolidated Press,
54 Park Street Sydney
Distributed by Network Distribution Company,
54 Park Street Sydney
Distributed in the U.K. by Australian Consolidated Press (UK)
Ltd (0604) 760 456. Distributed in Canada
by Whitecap Books Ltd (604) 980 9852. Distributed in South
Africa by Intermag (011) 493 3200.

■ ■ ■

Soft Furnishings

Includes index
ISBN 0 949128 34 1

1.Household linens. 2. Sewing.
(Series: Australian Women's Weekly
Home Library
646.21

■ ■ ■

© A C P 1991

■ ■ ■

COVER: Divan Cover and Valance, page 60, with Square
Cushions and Plain Bolster, page 28.
OPPOSITE: Striped Table Set, page 66.
BACK COVER: Clockwise from top left: Austrian Blind,
page 118, Gathered Lampshade, page 87, Tie-On Cover for
Director's Chair, page 50.

Soft Furnishings

Adding individual touches to a room can make an enormous difference. Brighten a window with a soft, billowing blind, transform a sofa with a cheery loose cover and matching cushions or sew a delicate sheet set complete with lacy pillowcases. This book, with its easy-to-follow instructions, shows you how simple it can be to redecorate; a generous bow, a tasselled trim or a practical, but pretty, tie can immediately liven up a weary piece of furniture or fabric. It really is easy when you know how!

Fabric and lace: Mr Tablecloth

BED LINEN

Luxurious bed linen can be yours for little cost, with a minimum of sewing skill and by making use of inexpensive, appealing cotton fabrics.

We give instructions for all the basics – fitted sheets, flat sheets, quilt covers and pillowcases. You will need to use sheeting, or very wide fabric for the sheets, but pillowcases can be made from almost any fabric, providing it is comfortable against the skin and it launders well.

Also included are tips on how to pretty up pillowcases, personalise a quilt cover and brighten a room with an easy bed canopy.

LEFT: White Bed Linen Set including fitted sheet, flat sheet with lace inset, quilt cover, pillowcases with lace edging and European pillowcases with lace edging.

WHITE BED LINEN SET

FLAT SHEET WITH LACE INSET

2.7m x 180cm-wide or 230cm-wide sheeting
(for single bed)
2.7m x 230cm-wide sheeting (for double bed)
2.7m x 250cm-wide sheeting (for queen bed)
2.8m x 250cm-wide sheeting (for king bed)
6cm-wide double edge Battenburg lace (length; to fit
width of sheet, plus 2cm)
thread

Finished size: Single 180cm x 254cm; double 230cm x 254cm; queen 266cm x 250cm; king 276cm x 250cm.

Note. Mattress sizes vary. Check measurements of your mattress before purchasing fabric. Maximum width of sheeting fabric available is usually 250cm; if making sheets for queen and king beds and wider fabric is available, it may be preferable.

Cut fabric for sheet: Single 265cm x 182cm (or 180cm if using 180cm-wide sheeting); double 265cm x 230cm; queen 268cm x 250cm; king 278cm x 250cm.

Turn under and stitch 1cm hems on raw edges of sheet.

FOR SINGLE AND DOUBLE SHEETS. Turn under and stitch another 7cm hem at upper edge and another 2cm at lower edge.

Hem each end of lace.

Pin lace across upper edge of sheet, just below 7cm hem. Stitch in place using zigzag or straight stitch. Carefully cut fabric away from behind lace. Neaten raw edges of fabric.

FOR QUEEN AND KING SHEETS. Hem each end of lace.

Cut off a 10cm-wide strip across sheet top. Spread sheet and cut-off strip 5cm apart, pin lace between fabric pieces, over raw edges. Stitch in place using straight stitch or zigzag. Turn over 5cm on top edge of sheet, stitch to form a hem. If 260cm-wide sheeting is available, queen and king bed sheets can be made as for double.

China: and frames: Home and Garden

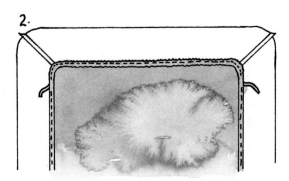

Cut two pieces of elastic the width of the mattress. Thread elastic pieces through casing at the top and bottom of sheet (diagram 2). Secure ends of elastic with stitching. Handstitch opening closed.

FITTED SHEET

1.4m x 230cm-wide sheeting (for single bed)
1.8m x 230cm-wide sheeting (for double bed)
2m x 250cm-wide sheeting (for queen bed)
2.3m x 250cm-wide sheeting (for king bed)
6mm-wide elastic (length; twice width of mattress)
thread

To fit mattress size: Single 91cm x 187cm x 20cm; double 137cm x 187cm x 20cm; queen 153cm x 203cm x 20cm; king 180cm x 203cm x 20cm. 1cm seam allowance is included. (Mattress sizes vary. To calculate correct sheet size, multiply the mattress depth by two and add this measurement, plus desired tuck-in allowance, to mattress length and width measurements.)

Mark a 20cm square at each corner of fabric. Cut out each square.

With right sides together, pin and stitch along cut edges (diagram 1). Trim and neaten seam.

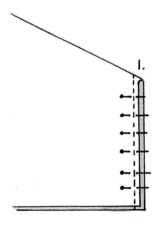

Neaten raw edges of sheet, then turn under 1cm all around to form a casing. Stitch along casing edge, leaving an opening in stitching at each corner.

QUILT COVER

2.9m x 230cm-wide sheeting (for single bed)
3.7m x 230cm-wide sheeting (for double bed)
4.3m x 230cm-wide sheeting (for queen bed)
5m x 230cm-wide sheeting (for king bed)
8 buttons
thread

Finished size: Single 140cm x 210cm; double 180cm x 210cm; queen 210cm x 210cm; king 245cm (width) x 210cm.

NOTE. We used damask fabric. Fabric quantities have been calculated using the most economical cutting method. Allow extra for patterned fabric with one-way design.

Cut two fabric pieces for cover: Single 142cm x 218cm; double 182cm x 218cm; queen 212cm x 218cm; king 247cm x 218cm. 1cm seam allowance is included.

Turn in and stitch a 1cm hem along one short end of each piece for single, double and queen cover, and along one long end of each piece for king cover (this will be the bottom edge of quilt).

Pin top and bottom cover, right sides together and matching hemmed edges. Stitch around the three raw edges. Trim and neaten seams. Turn right side out, press.

Turn in another 6cm along bottom edge, hem then topstitch. Press.

Make eight evenly spaced buttonholes along hemmed edge of top of cover, stitch buttons on bottom of cover to correspond.

RIGHT: Quilt Cover.

EUROPEAN PILLOWCASE WITH LACE EDGING

70cm x 150cm-wide fabric (we used damask)
3.4m x 10cm-wide single edge Battenburg lace
2.2m x 6cm-wide double edge Battenburg lace
thread

Finished size: 65cm square plus lace.

Cut one 67cm square piece fabric for front. Cut one 67cm x 45cm and one 67cm x 38cm piece fabric for back. Cut four 85cm pieces single edge lace and four 55cm pieces double edge lace. 1cm seam allowance is included.

Turn under and stitch a 1cm hem along one 67cm edge of each back piece. Turn under another 1cm on each piece and topstitch. Overlap large back piece 12cm over small back piece, tack edges together.

Pin and stitch single edge lace pieces, right sides together, mitring corners as shown in Pillowcase with Lace Edging (diagram 1) on page 9. Pin and stitch lace around front, raw edges and right sides together, as shown in Pillowcase with Lace Edging (diagram 2).

With right sides together, stitch double edge lace pieces together to form a square, mitring corners as before. Pin lace square to front pillowcase approximately 10cm in from edge, zigzag or handstitch in position.

With right sides together, pin back to front, over lace. Stitch, trim and neaten seam. Remove tacking, turn right side out.

PILLOWCASE WITH LACE EDGING

1m x 115cm-wide or 50cm x 180cm-wide fabric (we used damask)
2.9m x 6cm-wide single edge Battenburg lace thread

Finished size: 73cm x 48cm plus lace.

Cut one 75cm x 50cm piece fabric for front and one 78cm x 50cm piece fabric for back. Cut one 50cm x 20cm piece fabric for flap. Cut two 85cm and two 60cm pieces lace. 1cm seam allowance is included.

Turn under and stitch a 2cm hem along one 50cm edge of flap piece, then turn under another 2cm and topstitch.

Stitch lace pieces together to form a rectangle to fit front, mitring corners (diagram 1). With right sides and raw edges together, pin and stitch lace around front.

Turn in a 2cm hem along one 50cm edge of back piece, then turn under another 2cm and topstitch.

With right sides together, pin back to front around three raw edges.

Pin flap over back at open end of pillowcase, aligning raw edges and leaving hemmed edge of back free. Stitch all around pillowcase, trim and neaten seam. Turn right side out.

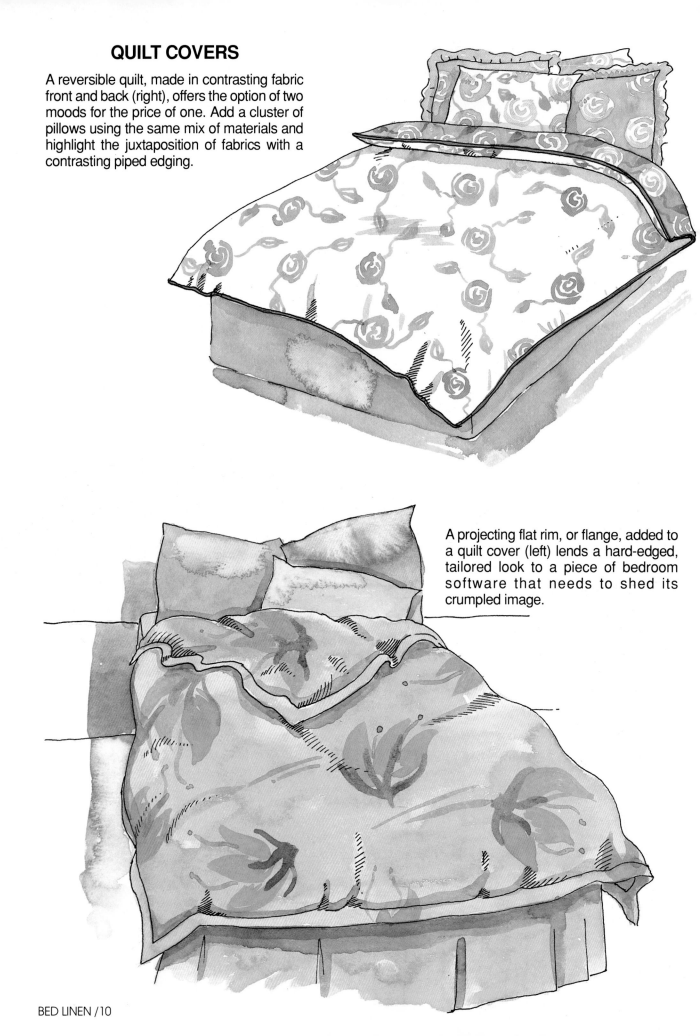

QUILT COVERS

A reversible quilt, made in contrasting fabric front and back (right), offers the option of two moods for the price of one. Add a cluster of pillows using the same mix of materials and highlight the juxtaposition of fabrics with a contrasting piped edging.

A projecting flat rim, or flange, added to a quilt cover (left) lends a hard-edged, tailored look to a piece of bedroom software that needs to shed its crumpled image.

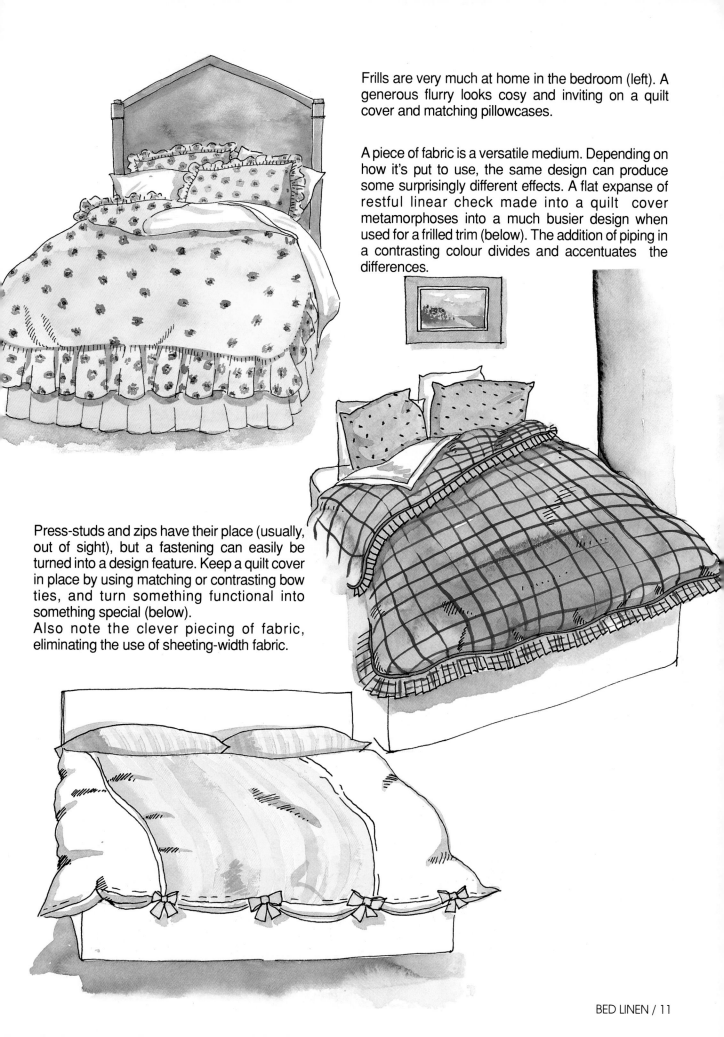

Frills are very much at home in the bedroom (left). A generous flurry looks cosy and inviting on a quilt cover and matching pillowcases.

A piece of fabric is a versatile medium. Depending on how it's put to use, the same design can produce some surprisingly different effects. A flat expanse of restful linear check made into a quilt cover metamorphoses into a much busier design when used for a frilled trim (below). The addition of piping in a contrasting colour divides and accentuates the differences.

Press-studs and zips have their place (usually, out of sight), but a fastening can easily be turned into a design feature. Keep a quilt cover in place by using matching or contrasting bow ties, and turn something functional into something special (below).
Also note the clever piecing of fabric, eliminating the use of sheeting-width fabric.

SHEETS

A plain sheet or pillowcase is enlivened by sewing a contrasting strip of fabric along the top edge or side (right). The strip can match the pattern of the bedroom curtains or other furnishings in the room, or simply accent the overall colour scheme. Patterned bed linen can be trimmed in the same way, either with a plain fabric of a different texture (satin on cotton, for example), or with a cheerful print that gives the finished item a richer, more sumptuous appearance.

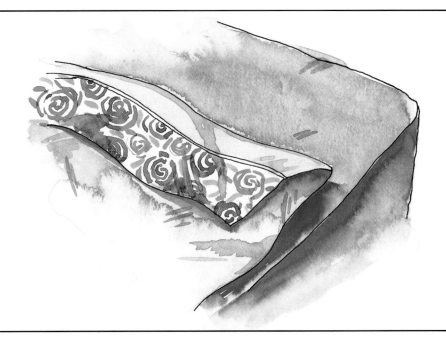

BASIC INSTRUCTIONS FOR MAKING PLAIN PILLOWCASES

PILLOWCASE IN ONE PIECE

50cm x 180cm-wide fabric
thread

Finished size: 73cm x 48cm.

Cut a 165cm x 50cm fabric piece. 1cm seam allowance is included.

Stitch a 1cm hem on one narrow end of fabric.

Turn under 1cm and then 2cm on the other end of fabric, stitch. With right sides of fabric together, fold under 73cm of this end, press.

Fold remaining 15cm of flap over 2cm-hemmed edge. Pin and stitch along both sides (see diagram).

Trim and neaten seam. Turn right side out, press.

AMERICAN-STYLE PILLOWCASE

This pillowcase has a hemmed opening with no flap.
50cm x 180cm-wide fabric
thread

Finished size: 73cm x 48cm.

Cut a 168cm x 50cm-wide fabric piece for pillowcase. 1cm seam allowance is included.

Fold fabric in half across width. Stitch a seam along both long sides. Trim and neaten seams.

Turn under 1cm around open edge of pillowcase. Turn under and stitch a 10cm hem around same edge (see diagram).

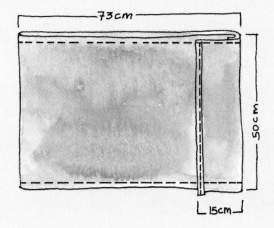

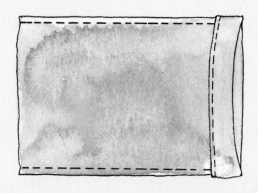

Ready-made sheets look as though they're custom-made when decorated with a little hand embroidery (right). A wavy line of running stitch or stem stitch is easily executed by the novice sewer, while those more competent with a needle could try numerous stitches such as feather, fern, chain or satin.

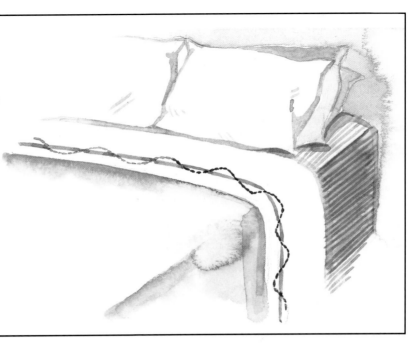

PILLOWCASE WITH SCALLOPED EDGE

1.8m x 115cm-wide fabric
small piece cardboard
dressmaker's chalk
thread

Finished size: 91cm x 66cm (including border).

Cut one 75cm x 50cm piece fabric for front. Cut two 50cm x 43cm pieces fabric for back. Cut two 99cm x 22cm fabric strips and two 72cm x 22cm fabric strips for scalloped edges. 1cm seam allowance is included.

Fold 22cm-wide strips in half lengthways, right sides together. Press.

Make a cardboard scallop edged template using a glass to mark edge (diagram 1). Draw four or five scallops onto cardboard. Mark scallops onto folded edge of fabric strip by tracing around cardboard pattern with dressmaker's chalk.

Stitch along scallop markings and trim next to stitching. Clip into points between each scallop, turn right side out and press.

With right sides together, stitch scalloped strips to edges of front piece, positioning scallops evenly and mitring corners following instructions for Pillowcase with Lace Edging on page 9. Trim and neaten seams.

Fold under and press 1cm hem along one 50cm edge of each back piece, fold under another 2cm and stitch close to edge. Overlap back pieces approximately 5cm to form 75cm x 50cm piece, tack centre edges together.

With right sides together, place back over front, with scalloped border facing centre of pillowcase. Pin and stitch around edges. Trim and neaten seams.

Remove tacking stitches and turn pillowcase right side out.

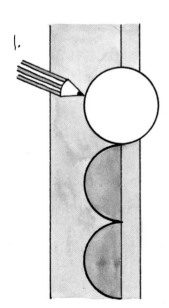

PILLOWCASE WITH MAUVE BOWS

73cm x 48cm white pillowcase
60cm mauve satin fabric
cardboard (cut to size of pillowcase)
thread

Finished size: 73cm x 48cm.

Cut four 65cm x 10cm strips satin fabric for bows. 1cm seam allowance is included.

Fold in half lengthways, right sides together. Pin and machine stitch along 65cm edge. Turn right side out, press and tie into bows. Cut ends diagonally, turn in ends, slip-stitch closed.

Cut two 51cm x 4.5cm and two 30cm x 4.5cm strips fabric for border. Press under 1cm along both long edges of strips.

Place cardboard inside pillowcase to make pinning easier. Pin long strips 10cm in from longest sides of pillowcase, tack.

Pin two shorter strips 10cm from opening and base seam of pillowcase, tack. Turn ends under to form neat corners. Machine stitch strips in place.

Handstitch bows at each corner of border.

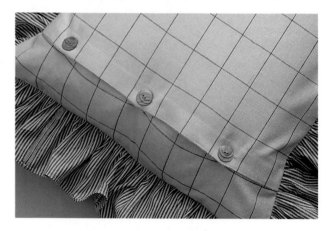

BUTTONED PILLOWCASE WITH FRILL

1m x 90cm-wide checked fabric
50cm x 90cm-wide striped fabric
three buttons
thread

Finished size: 93cm x 68cm (including frill).

Cut one 75cm x 50cm piece checked fabric for front pillowcase. Cut one 68cm x 50cm piece and one 50cm x 18cm piece checked fabric for back pillowcase. Cut four strips striped fabric 90cm x 12cm for frill. 1cm seam allowance is included.

Press under 1cm along one 50cm edge of each back section. Press under another 3cm and stitch.

Stitch three evenly spaced buttonholes along edge of larger back piece. Stitch buttons onto the smaller back

ABOVE: Pillowcase with Mauve Bows.
ABOVE RIGHT: Buttoned Pillowcase with Frill.
Above: Book and pencil: Balmain Linen and Lace. Above Right: China: Home and Garden.
Tray and mat: Balmain Linen and Lace

piece to correspond. Button back pieces together.

With right sides together, stitch three frill strips together at 12cm edges.

Stitch a small hem along one edge of frill. Stitch two rows of gathering on other edge. Pull up gathers to fit pillowcase.

With right sides together, pin and tack frill to front pillowcase matching raw edges.

With frill facing centre of pillowcase, pin back pieces over front, right sides together (see diagram).

Tack, stitch and neaten seam, turn right side out and press.

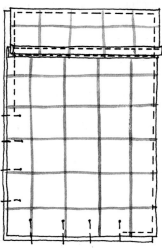

PILLOWCASE WITH HAND-APPLIQUE

73cm x 48cm white pillowcase
10cm x 6 different coloured lightweight cotton fabrics
(we used 3 greens, 1 pink, 1 blue and 1 yellow)
water-soluble pen or dressmaker's pencil
thread

Finished size: 73cm x 48cm.

Trace all pattern pieces using actual size pattern at right.

Place each pattern on right side of appropriate coloured fabric. Trace around shapes using water-soluble pen or dressmaker's pencil.

Cut out pieces adding extra 5mm around pencil lines.

Cut one of each piece unless otherwise indicated on pattern. Turn under 5mm and hand tack, clipping curves where necessary. You will need to gather the tacking stitches around curves to press hem flat. Clip allowances at corners (diagram 1).

For points on leaves, fold before tacking around edges (diagram 2). Press each piece.

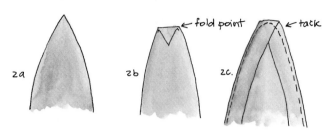

Position flowers and leaves near open end of pillowcase front (diagram 3). Pin and tack by hand, placing stem ends behind flowers and grass.

Stitch to pillowcase using small slip-stitches.

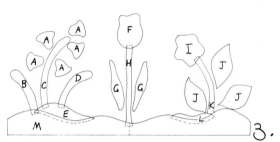

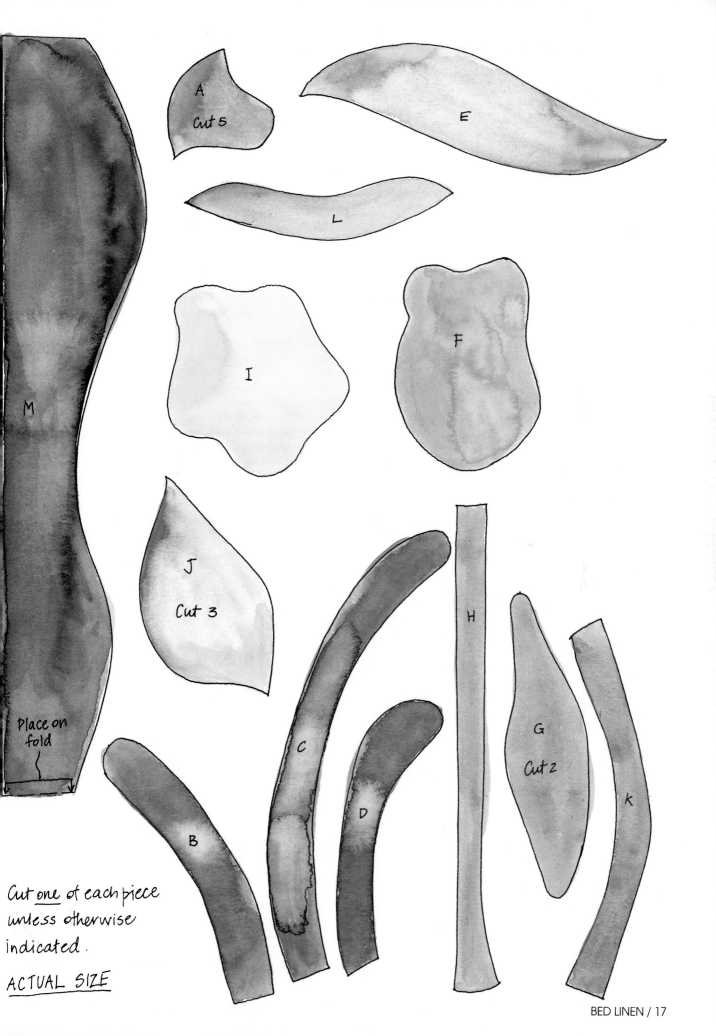

A
Cut 5

E

L

I

F

M

J
Cut 3

Place on fold

B

C

D

H

G
Cut 2

K

Cut <u>one</u> of each piece unless otherwise indicated.

ACTUAL SIZE

PILLOWCASE WITH BOW APPLIQUE

73cm x 48cm white pillowcase
20cm x 115cm-wide yellow cotton fabric
35cm white cotton fabric (we used pique)
1.25m x 1cm-wide ribbon
1.5m lace
20cm fusible webbing
water-soluble pen or dressmaker's pencil
thread
cardboard (cut to size of pillowcase)

Finished size: 73cm x 48cm.

Cut 32cm x 27cm rectangle white cotton fabric for applique background. 1cm seam allowance is included.

Apply webbing to 20cm strip yellow fabric. Trace actual size bow pattern below onto yellow fabric using water-soluble pen or dressmaker's pencil. Draw 27cm x 4cm band onto yellow fabric for ribbon piece, making 27cm lines slightly wavy. Cut out pieces.

Fuse ribbon piece and bow onto background fabric. Use close zigzag (satin stitch) to machine stitch around design.

Place cardboard inside pillowcase to make pinning easier. Pin and tack appliqued piece onto centre front of pillowcase.

Pin and tack lace around the edge of appliqued piece, pleating small tucks in lace at each corner.

Pin and sew ribbon in place over raw edge of lace.

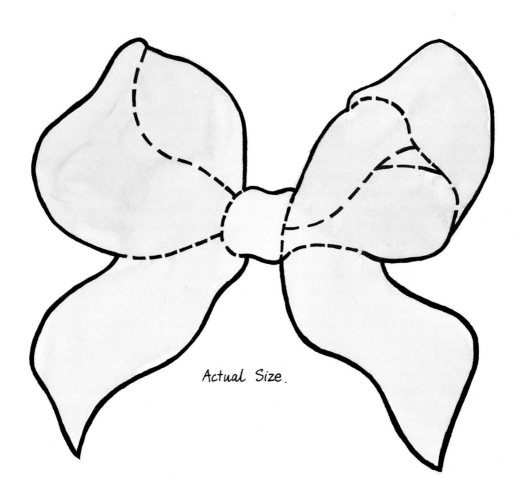

Actual Size.

PILLOWCASE WITH THREE TIES

1m x 115cm-wide fabric
thread

Finished size: 73cm x 48cm.

Cut two 75cm x 50cm pieces fabric for pillowcase. Cut two 50cm x 17cm pieces fabric for facing. Cut twelve 30cm x 3cm pieces fabric for ties. 1cm seam allowance is included unless otherwise stated.

Pin two tie pieces right sides together. Stitch leaving 5mm seam allowance and one short end open. Turn right side out. Repeat to make six ties.

With right sides of pillowcase pieces together, pin and sew around edges, leaving one short end open. Neaten seams, turn right side out.

Pin three ties along one edge of pillowcase, spacing them evenly. Pin remaining three ties on opposite edge in corresponding positions. Tack in place, aligning raw edges of ties with pillowcase edge.

Pin and stitch 17cm edges of facing, right sides together. Neaten one long edge of facing.

With right sides together, pin raw edge of facing over open end of pillowcase, over ties and matching side seams. Stitch (see diagram).

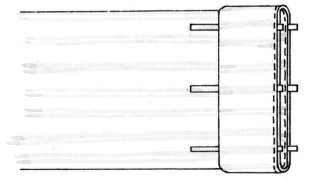

Trim seams, turn facing to inside and topstitch around open edge of pillowcase.

ABOVE: Pillowcase with Three Ties.
RIGHT: Pillowcase with Flange.
Above: Box and stationery: Balmain Linen and Lace

PILLOWCASE WITH FLANGE

1.4m x 115cm-wide fabric
thread, in contrasting and matching colour

Finished size: 89cm x 64cm (including flange).

Cut one 91cm x 66cm front pillowcase. Cut one 66cm x 54cm and one 66cm x 48cm back pillowcase. 1cm seam allowance is included.

Press under and stitch 3cm hem along one 66cm edge of each back piece. Overlap the smaller back section 5cm over larger and tack through all layers (diagram 1).

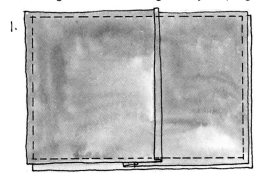

With right sides of front and back together, pin and sew seam. Turn right side out, press and remove tacking stitches.

Mark an 8cm line in from outside edge all around pillowcase and tack along markings. Sew along this line using contrasting thread and using close, wide zigzag stitch (diagram 2).

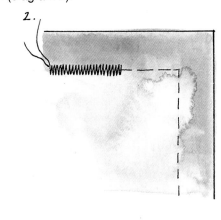

PILLOWCASE WITH PLEATED LACE AND BOWS

73cm x 48cm white pillowcase
2m x 5cm-wide white scallop edged cotton lace
1.8m x 5.5cm-wide white satin ribbon
thread

Finished size: 73cm x 48cm.

Fold lace into pleats, using the width of scallops as a guide to the width of pleats. Pin and tack pleats in place. Cut lace length in half.

Handstitch a length of pleated lace to open edge of pillowcase aligning scalloped edge with pillowcase edge and attaching it to the side without the flap.

Tack the second row of pleated lace 9cm from pillowcase edge, pointing scalloped edge in opposite direction.

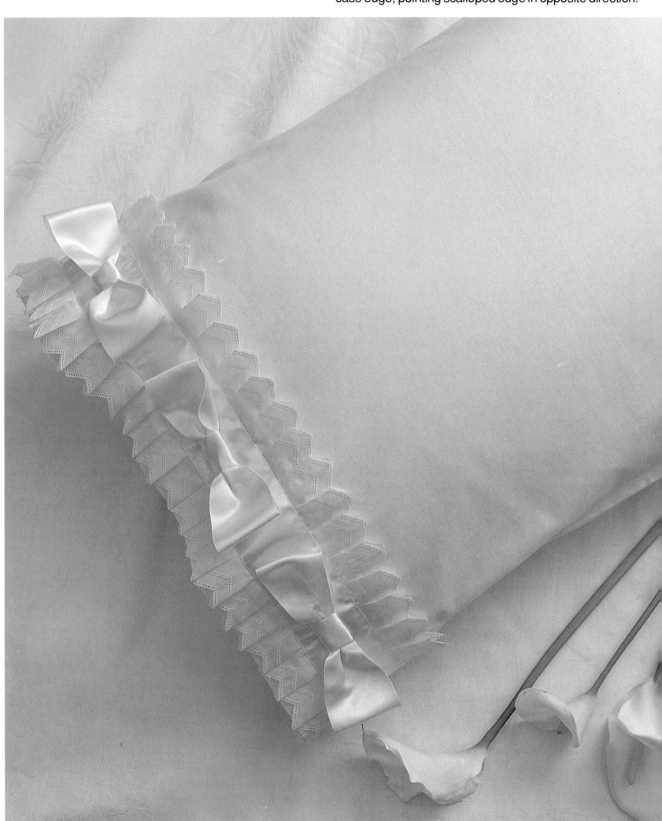

Neaten ends with 5mm handstitched hem.

Pin 50cm length of satin ribbon between two rows of lace, turning under 1cm at both ends. Machine stitch in place.

Cut three 35cm lengths and three 6cm lengths of satin ribbon for bows. Fold ends of longer strips to centre so they meet at centre back. Overlap slightly and secure with tacking stitches (diagram 1).

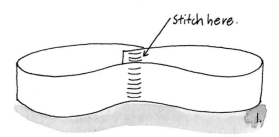

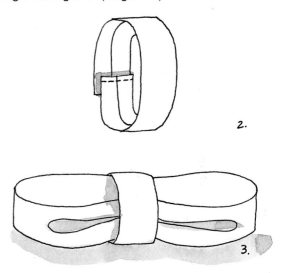

Turn under sides of 6cm lengths to form 3cm width (diagram 2). Form into loop by wrapping around bow and tacking ends together (diagram 3).

Position bows evenly along satin ribbon and stitch in place.

China: Home and Garden

TENT CANOPY

Replace a traditional bedhead with an elegant canopy which lends a dramatic touch to the bedroom scene. This easily made canopy is suspended from a curtain pole; fabric can be full and gathered on the pole or the same width as the pole, giving a flat, tented effect.

Fix hooks to ceiling. Allow enough fabric to drape generously over the pole and down both sides of the bed.

For a gathered canopy, fabric should be 1½-2 times the pole length. For a tented effect, make fabric the same width as pole length.

Hem all edges of the fabric. Fold fabric in half across width. Stitch a casing across folded edge wide enough to fit pole. Insert pole into casing. Finally, fix tie-back hooks to wall at either side of the bed, swathe a band of fabric around the canopy (or make your own tie-backs) and attach the bands to the hooks.

SHEER CANOPY

For the most romantic setting, suspend a sheer canopy over a bed dressed in lacy white linen. Netting or muslin fabric works wonderfully.

To make the canopy, fix a hook in the ceiling. Suspend a hoop from the hook with several lengths of strong thread (fishing line works well).

Measure around the bed to determine the width of the canopy, add 40cm extra for draping. Measure the fall of the canopy from ceiling to floor, add 20cm extra to drape fabric over the floor.

Stitch lengths of fabric into a tube to give required width and length, leave a front opening in one seam, below hoop. When stitching, use French seams to give a neat finish, without visible raw edges.

Lay canopy flat and mark the point where it falls over the hoop. Above this mark, trim the canopy edges so that they taper to a 20cm-wide point at ceiling level; this reduces the bulk at top of canopy. Stitch the trimmed edges of canopy together. Hem top edge and gather it. Stitch a loop of tape at the gathered top edge; the canopy will hang from this loop so make sure it is securely stitched.

Hem front opening and lower edge. Attach loop to hook, drape canopy over hoop and position the opening at the front.

CUSHIONS

Cushions are the simplest and most versatile soft furnishing addition. They can give a new look to a tired sofa, make a hard chair comfortable and inviting, or provide extra seating. Fabrics can range from durable handloomed cotton to boldly patterned chintz or delicate lace, and can be imaginatively trimmed with piping, tassels or frills. Fillings should be chosen carefully, keeping in mind the final use of the cushion. Feather filling makes soft, yet supportive, cushions which retain their shape and last for years; it is also the most expensive filling. A combination of feather and foam gives a less expensive but comfortable filling. Foam chips are cheap but tend to be lumpy and will crumble over time. A foam block can be cut to any size or shape to fit box style cushions and will hold its shape well. Polyester fibre is a fully washable, soft filling that will compact over time; it is slightly more expensive than foam.

LEFT: Divan Cover (instructions on page 60) with Square Cushions and Plain Bolsters.

SQUARE CUSHION

For each cushion:
60cm x 150cm-wide fabric
55cm square cushion insert
thread

Finished size: 55cm square.

Cut two cushion pieces 58cm square. Cut and join fabric to give a strip 1m x 13cm for bow. 1.5cm seam allowance is included.

Pin cushion pieces right sides together, stitch all around leaving a 35cm opening on one side. Turn right side out, press.

Fill with cushion insert, slip-stitch opening closed.

Fold bow strip lengthways, right sides together. Trim ends diagonally. Stitch along raw edges leaving a small opening in centre. Turn right side out, slip-stitch opening closed, press.

Tie into a bow and handstitch onto cushion.

PLAIN BOLSTER

For each bolster:
70cm x 120cm-wide fabric
40cm zipper
1.4m piping cord
70cm x 120cm-wide fabric (for insert)
polyester fibre filling
thread

Finished size: 61cm x 21cm.

Cut one 69cm x 64cm piece for bolster. Cut two 24cm-diameter circles for ends. 1.5cm seam allowance is included.

Apply piping around edge of each end piece following instructions for piping on page 125 (we cut our striped fabric to cover piping cord on the straight grain rather than on the bias).

Bring the 69cm edges of bolster piece together. Pin and stitch leaving a 40cm opening in seam centre for zipper. Neaten seams and press flat, turn right side out.

Insert zipper following instructions on page 126. Open zipper, turn bolster wrong side out.

Pin ends to bolster, right sides together, placing pins next to stitching line. Stitch, neaten seams, turn right side out.

Cut and make insert in same way as bolster, omitting piping and zipper. Turn right side out, fill with fibre filling and slipstitch opening closed. Place insert into bolster and close zipper.

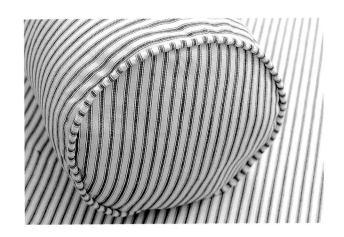

ROUND CUSHION WITH FRILL AND PIPING

1m x 115cm-wide fabric
2.7m purchased bias binding (for piping) *or* make your own bias binding following instructions
on page 125)
2.7m narrow piping cord
41cm round cushion insert
30cm zip
thread

Finished size: 54cm diameter.

Cut cushion pattern using a 42cm square of paper. Fold paper into quarters. Pin one end of a string to centre of paper, tie a pencil onto other end of string 21cm from pin. Draw a quarter circle with 21cm radius (diagram 1).

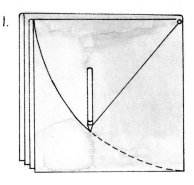

Cut cushion front using this pattern piece. Fold pattern in half and add 2cm along straight edge (diagram 2) to make back pattern. Cut two back pieces. 1cm seam allowance is included.

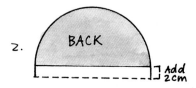

Cut a 16cm-wide fabric strip twice the cushion circumference measurement. (Our strip for a 40cm diameter cushion was 264cm long.)

Stitch frill strips right sides together at ends to give a continuous loop, and press seams open. Fold in half lengthways, wrong sides together, to make a double fabric frill, press. Fold frill into quarters, mark quarters with pins at raw edge.

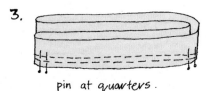

pin at quarters.

Stitch a row of gathering from one pin to the next, leaving a long thread at each pin. Make a second row of gathering stitches.

Apply piping to cushion front following instructions on page 125.

Fold front into quarters and mark with pins. Pull up gathers on frill matching each "pin to pin" length to each front quarter. Tie threads in a figure-eight around each pin to hold gathers in place.

Pin frill onto cushion front over piping, placing pins on wrong side of cushion front along stitching line. Tack, machine stitch using zipper foot.

Press under 2cm on straight edge of each back piece. Neaten raw edges and insert zipper following instructions on page 126. Open zipper.

With right sides together, pin back to front aligning raw edges. Stitch, trim and neaten seam. Turn right side out, press.

PIPED SQUARE CUSHION

70cm x 120cm-wide fabric or
1.1m x 115cm-wide fabric
2.1m purchased bias binding (for piping) or
make your own bias binding following instructions
on page 125)
2.1m piping cord
49cm square cushion insert
three buttons
thread

Finished size: 48cm square.

Cut one 50cm square piece of fabric for front. Cut one 50cm x 48cm piece of fabric for upper back and one 50cm x 21cm piece of fabric for lower back. 1cm seam allowance is included.

Fold under 6cm along one 50cm edge of each back piece to form self facing. Neaten raw edge of each facing.

Make three evenly spaced buttonholes along folded edge of upper back piece. Stitch three buttons onto lower back piece to correspond, button pieces together.

Apply piping to front cushion piece following instructions on page 125.

Pin back to front over piping, right sides together, placing pins on wrong side of front along stitching line, tack. Machine stitch using zipper foot. Trim corners and seams. Turn right side out, press.

RIGHT: Piped Square Cushion.

BUTTONED CUSHION

1m x 120cm-wide fabric
2.4m purchased bias binding (for piping) *or*
make your own bias binding following instructions
on page 125)
2.4m narrow piping cord
two buttons
quilting thread
polyester fibre filling
thread

Finished size: 35cm diameter.

Cut one 37cm diameter circular cushion pattern, measuring an 18.5cm radius, following method described in Round Cushion with Frill and Piping on page 29.

Cut two circles of fabric using pattern. Cut one 118cm x 8cm strip for cushion wall. 1cm seam allowance is included.

If using self fabric bias, make 240cm bias binding following instructions on page 125. Apply piping to cushion front and back, following instructions on page 125.

With right sides together, stitch 8cm edges of cushion wall together. Trim, neaten and press seam open.

Pin one edge of wall to cushion front over piping, right sides together. Machine stitch using zipper foot.

Pin other edge of wall to cushion back, right sides together, leaving opening for fibre filling. Turn right side out. Insert fibre filling. Slip-stitch opening closed.

TO COVER BUTTONS. Cut circles of fabric 2cm larger than button. Run gathering threads around edges of circles. Place small amount of fibre filling in centre of circle and position button on top. Draw up gathering threads and tie off ends (diagram 1).

Use quilting thread and large needle to sew a few stitches through centre of cushion, stitching through all layers and pulling thread taut (diagram 2). Stitch buttons in centre of cushion over stitches.

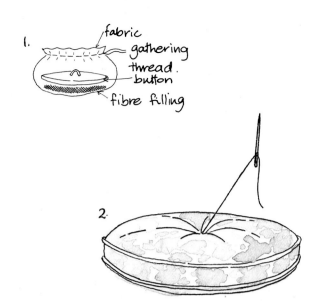

BOLSTER WITH GATHERED ENDS

60cm x 115cm-wide fabric
1.1m purchased bias binding (for piping) *or*
make your own bias binding following instructions
on page 125)
1.1m narrow piping cord
60cm x 115cm-wide fabric (for cushion insert)
two 3cm diameter buttons
30cm zipper
polyester fibre filling
thread

Finished size: 54cm x 20cm.

Cut one 56cm square bolster piece and two 56cm x 11cm end pieces. 1cm seam allowance is included.

Apply piping to 2 parallel sides of bolster piece following instructions on page 125.

Fold bolster piece in half, right sides together, so piping is at each end. Pin and stitch along length, leaving 30cm opening in seam for inserting zipper. Turn right side out.

Insert zipper following instructions on page 126. Turn bolster wrong side out.

With right sides together, stitch 11cm edges of one end piece. Repeat with remaining end piece.

Pin end pieces over each end of bolster piece, right sides together and over piping. Stitch, trim, neaten raw edges (diagram 1).

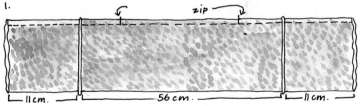

Handstitch a gathering thread around raw edges of end pieces. Pull up gathers and knot threads. Turn right side out (diagram 2).

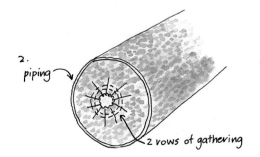

Left: Rug: Home and Garden

TO COVER BUTTONS. Follow method described in Buttoned Cushion on previous page.

Pin covered buttons to centre of each end, over small openings. Handstitch in place by slip-stitching the fabric cover of button to bolster fabric.

BOLSTER INSERT. Cut one 57cm square and two 25cm diameter circles from fabric. (Bread and butter plates can be used to trace circles).

Fold square in half, right sides together. Pin and stitch along length leaving opening for filling. Press seam open.

With right sides together, pin and stitch circles to each end. Turn right side out, insert fibre filling and slip-stitch opening closed.

Place insert inside cover and close zip.

TARTAN CUSHION WITH PLEATED FRILL

1.60m x 115cm-wide tartan or check fabric
two buttons
40cm square cushion insert
thread

Finished size: 59cm square.

Cut one 39cm square front piece. (We cut our fabric on the bias.) Cut two 39cm x 25.5cm back pieces. Cut four 13.5cm x 115cm frill lengths, matching pattern. 1cm seam allowance is included.

Join frill lengths at ends to give a continuous strip and stitch a 1.5cm hem along one long edge.

Form pleats along strip by folding fabric at equal intervals. Press, pin and tack pleats in place. (Our pleats were 2.5cm wide but they will need to be sized to suit the pattern on the fabric.)

To attach pleated frill to cushion front, begin at a corner and pin along straight edge. Concertina three pleats into one at each corner so they fan out (see diagram). Continue pinning pleats to front.

At final corner, measure fabric required for three pleats and joining seam. Trim off excess fabric.

Before pinning corner pleats in position, stitch fabric ends together. Pin remaining pleats and stitch in place.

Turn under 5cm along one 39cm edge of each back piece to form self facing. Neaten raw edge of each facing.

Make two evenly spaced buttonholes along folded

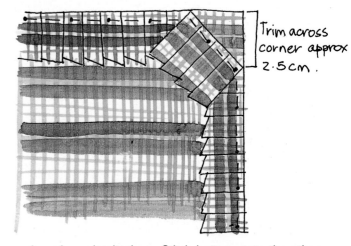

Trim across corner approx 2.5cm.

edge of one back piece. Stitch buttons onto the other back piece to correspond. Button back pieces together.

With right sides together, pin back to front over pleats, with pleats facing towards centre. Machine stitch around edges. Turn right side out and press.

LEFT: Bolster with Gathered Ends.
ABOVE: Tartan Cushion with Pleated Frill.
Left: Rug: Home and Garden. Above: Chair: Montague North. Cloth: Home and Garden

Fabric: Les Olivades

SQUAB CUSHION

1.3m x 115cm-wide fabric
polyester fibre filling
thread

Finished size: 56cm diameter, or to fit your chair.

To make a pattern for cushion, place paper on chair seat and trace outline. Add 1cm seam allowance all around outline and cut out pattern (our pattern had a 43cm diameter).

Use pattern to cut cushion top piece. Fold pattern in half and add 4cm along straight edges. Cut two cushion bottom pieces using pattern.

Cut three 17cm-wide frill strips making each strip the same length as the cushion top circumference (our cushion had a 129cm circumference). Cut four 20cm x 6cm ties. 1cm seam allowance is included.

Stitch frill strips together at 17cm ends to make a continuous loop. Fold in half lengthways, wrong sides together and press.

Fold strip into 1cm pleats and tack along raw edge. Pin pleated frill to top piece, right sides together, aligning raw edges.

Fold under 1cm along 20cm edges and one end of each tie piece. Fold in half lengthways, wrong sides together, topstitch along length and across one end. Position over frill, matching raw edges and spacing ties 25cm apart. Tack and stitch frill and ties in place (see diagram).

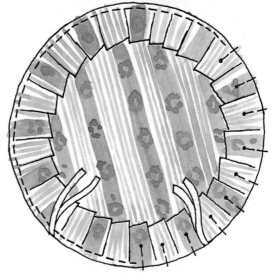

Fold under 2cm along straight edges of each bottom piece to form self facing. Neaten raw edge of each facing. Overlap bottom pieces to fit front, pin together.

Stitch top to bottom, right sides together, with ties and frill facing centre. Trim edges and turn cushion to right side through back opening. Insert fibre filling, handstitch back overlap closed.

HEART-SHAPED CUSHION

1.6m x 115cm-wide fabric
1.2m bias binding to match fabric (for piping) *or* make
your own bias binding following instructions
on page 125)
1.2m narrow piping cord
three buttons
40cm x 90cm-wide fabric (for cushion insert)
polyester fibre filling
thread

Finished size: 64cm x 55cm.

Cut heart-shaped cushion pattern following diagram (our cushion was 27cm from point to point). Cut one cushion front using this pattern. Cut two cushion back pieces by cutting pattern in half and adding 6cm to each straight edge. Cut three 115cm x 30cm strips of fabric for frill. 1cm seam allowance is included.

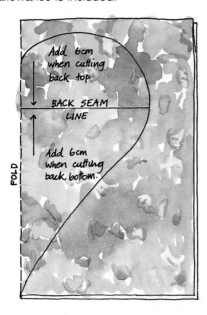

Stitch frill strips together at 30cm edges to make a continuous loop. Fold in half, wrong sides together, to make a double fabric frill, press.

Apply piping to front piece following instructions on page 125.

Machine stitch 2 rows gathering thread along raw edges of frill.

Pull up gathers on frill and pin to front over piping, matching raw edges. Machine stitch frill in place.

Fold under 4cm along straight edge of each back section to form self facing. Neaten raw edge of facing. Make three evenly spaced buttonholes along folded edge of upper back piece. Stitch three buttons onto lower back piece to correspond. Button back pieces together.

Pin back to front over frill and piping, right sides together, with frill facing centre. Machine stitch using zipper foot. Trim and clip seam, turn right side out, press.

Chair: Montague North. Plate: Home and Garden

CUSHION INSERT. Make in the same way as above using heart-shaped pattern, but cut pieces 2cm larger all around and omit frill and piping.

Place insert inside cover and button closed.

BUTTONED SQUAB CUSHION

1.2m x 115cm-wide fabric
four self-cover buttons
polyester fibre filling
two press studs
thread

Finished size: 56cm square, or to fit your chair.

Cut two 41cm square pieces of fabric or make pattern to fit your chair and cut fabric using pattern, see Squab Cushion on page 37. Round off two corners of each piece (front edge of cushion). Cut three 1m x 19cm pieces of fabric for frill strips. Cut four 10cm x 6cm pieces of fabric for ties. 1cm seam allowance is included.

Sew frill strips together at 19cm edges to give a continuous loop. Fold in half lengthways, wrong sides together, and press flat.

Stitch two rows of gathering along raw edge of frill. Pull up gathers.

Pin frill around edge of one cushion piece (top) aligning raw edges. Pull up gathers to fit, concentrate gathers at rounded corners. Tack and stitch (see diagram).

Fold under 1cm along 14cm edges and one end of each tie piece. Fold in half lengthways, wrong sides together, topstitch along length and across folded end.

Position two ties 5cm in from each back corner. Align raw edges of ties with raw edges of frill, pin and stitch.

With right sides together, pin bottom to top cushion piece over frill. Tack and stitch around edge, leaving 20cm opening between ties. Trim edges, turn right side out.

Insert fibre filling and handstitch opening closed.

Cover buttons following manufacturer's instructions. Using quilting thread and large needle, sew a few stitches through all layers at each button position, pulling thread taut. Stitch buttons over stitches.

Stitch press studs onto ties.

BELOW: Buttoned Squab Cushion.
RIGHT: Square Cushion with Frill.
Below: Chair: Montague North. Right: Chair: Montague North. Cup and saucer: Home and Garden

Fabric: Les Olivades

SQUARE CUSHION WITH FRILL

1.2m x 115cm-wide fabric
20cm extra fabric (for bow, optional)
three buttons
43cm square cushion insert
thread

Finished size: 64cm square.

Cut one 44cm square piece of fabric for front. Cut two 44cm x 29cm pieces of fabric for back. Cut a 24cm-wide frill strip twice the length of the cushion circumference. (Our strip for a 44cm square cushion was 352cm long.) 1cm seam allowance is included.

Stitch frill strip together at ends, right sides together.

Trim, neaten and press seams open.

Fold frill strip in half lengthways, wrong sides together, to make a double fabric frill. Press.

Fold frill into quarters and mark with pins at raw edge (diagram 1). Using the longest stitch on your machine, run a gathering thread from one pin to the next, leaving a long thread at each pin.

1.

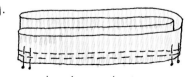

pin at quarters.

Make a second row of gathering stitches, like the first row. Pull up the gathers so that each "pin to pin" length matches each cushion side length. Tie threads in a figure-eight around pins to hold gathers in place.

Pin frill onto front, matching the four pins to the centres of each side of the cushion (diagram 2). Concentrate gathers at each corner. Machine stitch frill in place.

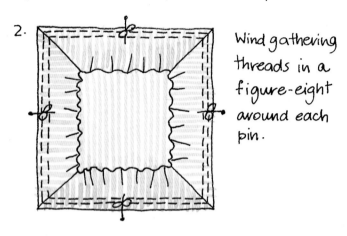

2.

Wind gathering threads in a figure-eight around each pin.

Fold under 6cm along one 44cm edge of each back piece to form self facing. Neaten raw edge of each facing.

Make three evenly spaced buttonholes along folded edge of one back piece. Stitch buttons to folded edge of other back piece to correspond and button pieces together.

With right sides together, pin back to front over frill, with finished frill edges facing centre.

Machine stitch, trim corners and neaten seams. Turn right side out, press.

BOW (optional). Cut a 90cm x 14cm strip of fabric. Fold in half lengthways, right sides together. Stitch along 90cm raw edge.

Cut ends diagonally, turn right side out, press. Tie into a bow, turn in ends and slip-stitch closed. Stitch bow in place on cushion.

PIPED CHAIR CUSHION

1.3m x 115cm-wide fabric
2.6m narrow piping cord
5cm-thick foam, cut to size of cushion
thread

Finished size: 40cm diameter, or to fit your chair.

Make pattern and cut fabric for top and bottom cushion pieces following the method described for Squab Cushion on page 37 (our pattern for cushion top was 43cm diameter). Cut two 65.5cm x 8cm pieces fabric for gusset (add extra length for larger cushion). Cut four 85cm x 13cm pieces fabric for bows. 1.5cm seam allowance is included.

Stitch ends of two bow pieces right sides together. Fold in half lengthways, right sides together, trim ends diagonally. Stitch along raw edges leaving a small opening in centre. Trim and neaten seams, turn right side out, slip-stitch opening closed. Repeat for other bow pieces.

Fold under 2cm along straight edge of each bottom piece to form self facing. Overlap pieces to fit top piece, pin bottom pieces together.

Make a bias strip for piping following instructions on page 125. Apply piping to edges of top and bottom, following instructions on page 125.

With right sides together, stitch ends of gusset pieces together to make a continuous loop. Pin and stitch one edge of gusset to back cushion piece, over piping, right sides and raw edges together. Stitch using zipper foot. Trim and neaten seams. Repeat to attach gusset to top piece.

Fold bow strips in half across width, press foldline. Position foldline at back of cushion in positions to suit chair, pin to gusset (our bows were 23cm apart). Hand-stitch in place, stitching along foldlines (see diagram).

Insert foam filling and handstitch back overlap closed.

RIGHT: Piped Chair Cushion.

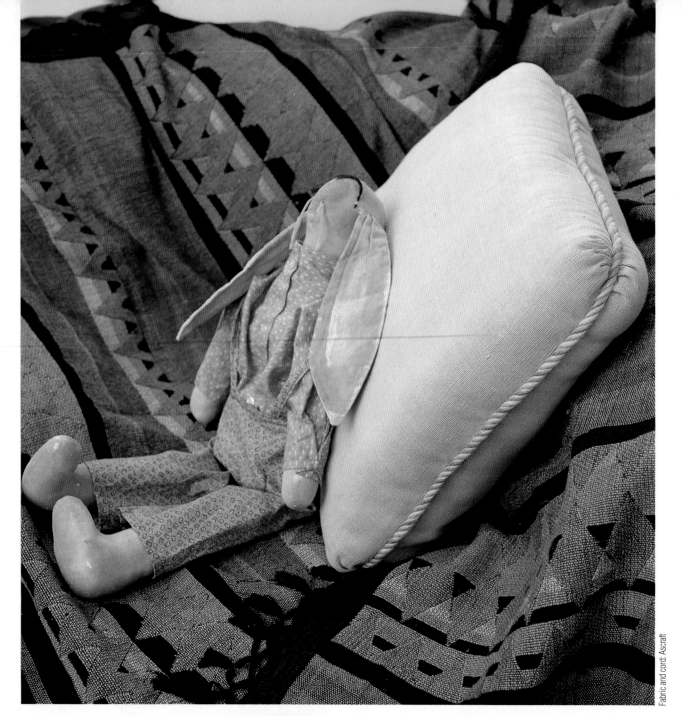

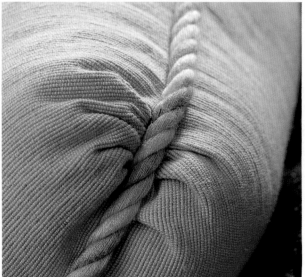

CUSHION WITH GATHERED CORNERS

50cm x 115cm-wide fabric
2.1m thick cord
polyester fibre filling
2.1m x 2cm-wide tape
thread

Finished size: 46cm square.

Cut two 50cm square pieces fabric for front and back cushion. 2cm seam allowance is included.

Measure 5cm along edge of cushion pieces from each corner. Measure and mark 2.5cm in diagonally from corners. Form a curve by drawing a line from one edge through the diagonal marking to the other edge.

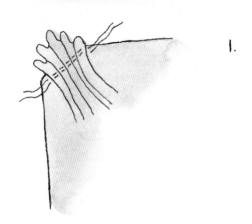

1.

Handstitch gathering stitches along marked curve and pull up stitches (diagram 1). Tie off threads firmly. Repeat for each corner.

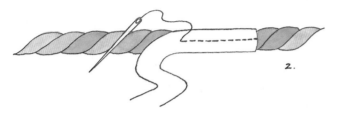

2.

3.

Handstitch cord to centre of tape (diagram 2) to make piping. Tack and stitch the piping (with tape attached) around the front cushion edges following instructions for piping on page 125 and overlapping ends of cord (diagram 3).

With right sides together, pin and tack cushion front to back. Stitch, leaving a 20cm opening in one side.

Turn right side out, insert fibre filling, stitch opening closed.

CUSHION WITH DIAGONAL FRONT PANELS AND TIES

60cm x 115cm-wide fabric
10cm x 90cm-wide contrasting fabric
40cm square cushion insert
thread

Finished size: 38cm square.

Cut 40cm square cushion pattern. Cut cushion back using this pattern piece. Fold pattern piece in half diagonally. Cut two fabric pieces for front using this pattern piece and adding 4cm along diagonal edge. Cut six 30cm x 6cm pieces fabric for ties. Using contrasting fabric, cut one curved 60cm x 10cm piece fabric for front flap (diagram 1). 1cm seam allowance is included unless otherwise stated.

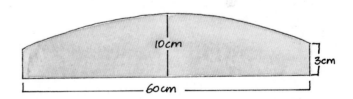

Fold one tie piece in half lengthways, right sides together. Cut one end diagonally, pin and stitch along raw edge and across diagonal end using 5mm seam allowance. Turn right side out and press. Repeat for remaining ties.

Press under 4cm along diagonal edge of each front piece to form self facing. Stitch narrow hems along facing edges.

Pin three ties on wrong side of diagonal edge of one front piece, spacing them evenly (ours were 11.5cm apart). Pin three ties on wrong side of diagonal edge of remaining front piece to correspond.

Pin straight edge of flap under diagonal edge of one front piece, with ties between cushion and flap. Topstitch next to the front diagonal edge, then topstitch 5mm away from first row of stitching. Turn in and stitch a narrow hem on the curved edge of flap. This piece will sit under the other front piece.

Pin front and back cushion pieces, right sides together. Stitch all around, slightly curving each corner. Trim and neaten seams, turn right side out and press.

Place cushion insert into cushion through front panel. Knot ties to close cushion.

CUSHION WITH SIDE TIES

70cm x 115cm-wide fabric
40cm square cushion insert
thread

Finished size: 38cm square.

Cut two 40cm square pieces fabric for front and back. Cut two 40cm x 14cm pieces fabric for front flaps. Cut two 40cm x 5cm pieces fabric for back facings. Cut twelve 30cm x 6cm ties. 1cm seam allowance is included unless otherwise stated.

Fold one tie piece in half lengthways, right sides together. Cut one end diagonally, pin and stitch along raw edge and diagonal end using 5mm seam allowance. Trim seams, turn right side out and press. Repeat for remaining ties.

Position three ties at two opposite edges of front and back cushions, with raw edges together. Space ties evenly (ours were 8.5cm apart). Pin and tack.

With right sides together, pin and stitch front flaps to each end of front cushion, over ties. Trim and neaten seam, turn flap to wrong side of cushion, press. Stitch back facings to back cushion piece, over ties, in same way as front flaps.

Stitch narrow hems on the raw edge of flaps and facings. Hem edges of back facings to cushion back. Tack sides of front flaps in place on front cushion.

With right sides together, pin and stitch front onto back cushion along side edges, stitching a rounded corner at each end. Trim and neaten seams, turn right side out and press.

Place cushion insert into cushion. Knot ties to close cushion.

LEFT: Cushion with Diagonal Front Panels and Ties.
ABOVE: Cushion with Side Ties.

Fabric: Ascraft

FURNITURE COVERS

Complicated upholstery is an art best left to professionals. However, simple projects such as recovering an upholstered seat can easily be done at home – you'll save money and give a new lease of life to tired looking furniture.

We show you how an ordinary director's chair becomes ready for dining room duty in a slip-on cover tied with sassy bows, and an old divan looks smart when skirted and piped with striped cotton. With a little more time and effort, loose sofa covers will reward; they give new elegance to jaded upholstery and make the luxury of seasonal covers affordable.

LEFT: Tie-On Cover for Director's Chair.

TIE-ON COVER FOR DIRECTOR'S CHAIR

2.2m x 115cm-wide fabric
thread

To calculate length of main fabric piece, measure from the floor at back of chair, to top of chair uprights, down inside back, from back of seat to front and down to the floor (see A on diagram 1). To calculate width of main fabric piece, measure across back of chair from outside edge of one upright to outside edge of the other (see B on diagram 1).

To calculate width and length of side pieces, measure from side edge of seat, up over arm and down to floor (see C on diagram 1) and from back of seat to front of seat (see D on diagram 1). Add 1cm seam allowance on all edges. Cut out one main piece and two side pieces. Cut four 70cm x 8cm pieces, for ties.

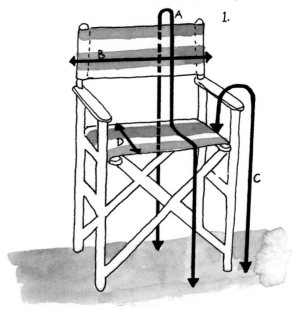

NOTE. Our main fabric piece measured 220cm x 59cm, and side pieces measured 89cm x 50cm (including seam allowance). Chair sizes may vary; check these measurements to make sure they fit your chair.

Place main fabric piece in position on chair, wrong side up. Place a pin at top of uprights, seat back and seat front to mark these positions. Pin fabric edges together from top of uprights to arms, pinning a 1cm seam allowance. Remove and stitch pinned seams.

Replace cover on chair; pins should be in correct positions. Pin narrow edge of each side piece to main piece, between back of seat and front of seat markings. Fold fabric over arm, pin side edges together from top of arm to point where side piece joins main piece at seat edge. From this point to floor, pin side piece to main piece; edges at floor level should be even. Remove cover and stitch pinned seams.

At top of each arm, pin a small seam across the folded edge at front, at right angles to the seam running down the front. Stitch and trim (diagram 2). Neaten all raw edges on seams. Neaten remaining raw edges, turn under and stitch a 1cm hem.

Neaten and stitch a 1cm hem on long edges and one narrow edge on tie pieces. Pin a tie to each side of main piece level with back of arms. Pin a tie to side piece at back to correspond. Stitch ties in place. Turn cover to right side, place cover over chair and tie bows at back.

TWO-PIECE DIRECTOR'S CHAIR COVER

60cm x 90cm-wide fabric (we used canvas)
thread
upholstery tacks or staple gun

Remove old cover, unpick seams on old cover and use it as a pattern for new cover. If there is no old cover, calculate width of back piece by measuring around one upright, across open frame and around other upright. Make depth of back piece as required.

Measure seat frame and add allowance to tack fabric at each side plus 1cm hem allowance to all edges.

NOTE. Our back piece measured 71cm x 19cm, seat piece measured 58cm x 41cm. Chair sizes may vary; check these measurements to make sure they will fit your chair.

Neaten and stitch a 1cm hem along all edges of back piece. Turn under and pin a 6cm casing on each side. Place back onto chair uprights, check fit, adjust casing if necessary. Remove back piece, double stitch casing in place (diagram 1).

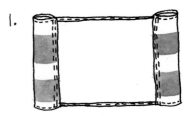

Replace back on chair, fix at desired height with tacks or staples in back of chair uprights.

Neaten and stitch a 1cm hem along all edges of seat piece. Place seat piece onto chair, pull side edges around to underside of seat frame. Check fit of seat piece, adjust if necessary. Fold frame closed and fix seat in place with tacks, or staples (diagram 2).

2.

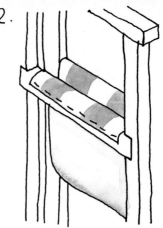

ONE-PIECE DIRECTOR'S CHAIR COVER

90cm x 90cm-wide fabric (we used canvas)
thread
upholstery tacks or staple gun

To calculate width of fabric piece, measure around one upright, across open frame and around other upright. To calculate length of fabric piece, measure from 3cm below upright, down chair inside back and, from back of seat to front of seat. Add 1cm seam allowance to all edges.

NOTE. Our fabric piece measured 85cm x 71cm. On each side, cut out a 12cm-wide curved section, 20cm below the top edge and 27cm long (see diagram). Chair sizes may vary; check these measurements to make sure they will fit your chair frame.

Neaten and stitch a 1cm hem along all edges of fabric including cut-out curved section at sides.

Turn under and pin a 6cm casing along side edge above cut-out section. Fit cover onto chair uprights, check fit, adjust casing if necessary. Remove cover, double stitch casing in place.

Replace cover on chair, pull side edges of seat around to underside of seat frame. Check fit of seat, trim at sides if necessary. Fix seat in place with tacks, or staples.

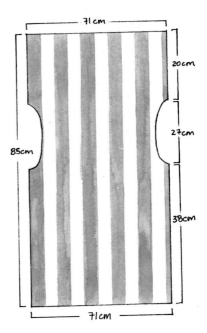

Fix back at desired height with tacks or staples in back of chair uprights.

Fabric: Whitehouse Interior Design

TAILORED LOOSE COVER FOR SOFA

fabric
piping cord
hooks and eyes *or* hook and loop tape
thread
dressmaker's chalk

NOTE. Each section of the loose cover is cut out in a rectangle roughly the right size. These pieces are pinned onto the sofa, then trimmed and pleated to fit exactly. They are then removed and stitched together, with piping added where necessary.

MEASURING. Remove seat cushions and carefully measure each section of the sofa, measuring at the longest and widest points (diagram 1). Inside arm should be measured from seat over arm to outside of arm, finishing either underneath scroll or halfway around scroll; use original upholstery lines as a guide.

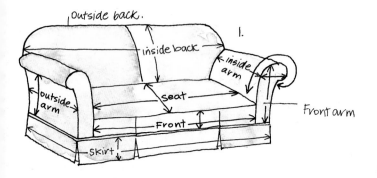

Record the shape and measurement of each piece and add 1.5cm seam allowance on all sides and a 15cm tuck-in allowance. Tuck-in allowance should be added where fabric tucks into seat or under cushions, for example, at lower edge of inside arm, lower edge of inside back, and at edges between inside arm and inside back.

Calculate and record skirt measurements, adding 10cm allowance for kick pleats at each corner of sofa. Also allow 10cm inserts, same width as skirt, for kick pleats at corners. If a gathered skirt or no skirt is required, see box on page 58.

CALCULATING FABRIC REQUIREMENTS. Draw a plan, marking in each separate piece, positioning it along the correct grain (diagram 2). Large pieces which are wider than the fabric width, need to be pieced and fabric pattern should be matched. In some areas, such as the inside back, if it is not possible to match the pattern, the seam joining the pieces can be piped.

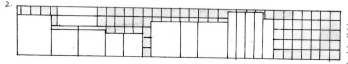

Candlesticks: Home and Garden

Fabric: Hermitage by John Kaldor

Smooth out fabric and check size. Trim fabric to sofa shape, leaving seam allowance and tuck-in allowance intact (diagram 3).

3.

Continue with inside arm and outside arm sections.

On scroll-armed sofas, trim tuck-in allowance between inside back and inside arm sections, so full allowance is left on lower edge but tapered to 1.5cm seam allowance at top edge (diagram 4).

4.

Seams at both sides of outside back piece should be left open to enable cover to be removed. Clip seam allowance around curves.

Pin the seat piece in position between the inside arms and back. For a pull-out sofa bed, the seat piece can be joined with hook and loop tape instead of stitching, to allow bed to unfold.

Add measurements for each piece and calculate fabric requirements. Add extra fabric for piping and cushions. Allow extra fabric for pattern matching.

CUTTING FABRIC. Cut out each fabric piece, placing it on the correct grain and matching fabric pattern wherever possible. Fabric motifs should be placed in the centre of each section. Pin an identifying label on each piece. Calculate and make required amount of piping (see piping instructions on page 125).

PIN FITTING. Mark centre of each section of the sofa and fabric pieces with chalk. Pin outside back piece to sofa, keeping crosswise grain parallel to floor and matching centres of sofa and fabric. Pieces can be pinned wrong side out, which makes stitching easier, or right side out if pattern placement needs to be checked (repinning will have to be done before stitching if pinned right side out).

Using chalk, mark stitching line on fabric. Pin inside back to sofa, and then pin the pieces together at adjoining seamlines.

Pin the front arm pieces next. For a scroll-armed sofa there will be fullness on the inside arm piece which needs to be pleated to fit the front arm piece. Position pleats evenly around arm, pin in place (diagram 5).

Place cover on sofa, check fit. Remove cover, neaten seams. Pin and stitch front panel in place.

Cut a facing strip twice as long as opening between outside back and outside arm and 5cm wide. Stitch facing around opening (diagram 6). Neaten raw edge and turn the facing along outside arm to inside of cover.

5.

6.

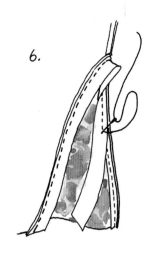

Remove cover, stitch seams of main pieces. Where seams are piped, stitch piping along seamline before stitching fabric pieces together (see instructions for piping on page 125).

Attach hooks and eyes or hook and loop tape to facing (diagram 7), positioning fastenings so edges of outside back and outside arm will align.

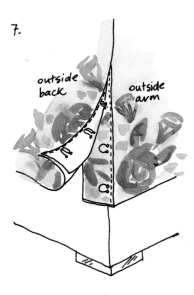

Stitch pleat inserts between each skirt length. Fold insert into a pleat, tack (diagram 8). Stitch piping around lower edge of sofa cover if desired. Stitch skirt in place over piping. Hem lower edge and ends of skirt.

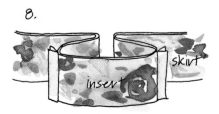

If sofa is box-shaped and has an extra strip between each main section, these should be pinned in place as you work.

Make cushions same size and shape as original sofa cushions, see Cushion chapter beginning on page 26.

GATHERED SKIRT FINISH

Cut skirt pieces depth required and twice the finished length. Stitch two rows of gathering along one long edge. Pull up gathers to fit sofa cover edge. Pin skirt edge along bottom edge of sofa cover, right sides together, concentrating extra gathers at corners. Stitch skirt to sofa cover, neaten edge. Stitch hem along lower edge of skirt (see diagram).

TIED-UNDER FINISH

If no skirt is required, a tied-under finish will hold the lower edge of the sofa cover in place. Measure and make cover sections for outside back, outside arms, front arms and front to fit to bottom edge of sofa.

Cut pieces to fit along each bottom section x about 20cm wide, for tie-under flaps. Stitch flaps to lower edge of each section, trim excess fabric so flaps clear the sofa feet. Neaten raw edges. Stitch a 1.5cm-wide casing along long edges of flaps. Thread a length of cotton tape through the casing on each flap. Fit cover to sofa, fold flaps under seat and tie in position with tape (see diagram).

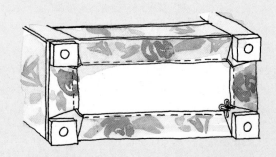

FURNITURE COVERS

A loose cover revitalizes that old sofa you can't afford to replace or re-upholster. Also, it protects an expensive one from wear and tear. Ideally, the fabric should be hard-wearing and hand or machine-washable. For a tie-on cover, make a feature of the bows that hold it in place (left). Extravagant bows turn a plain cover into a classic, and add a jaunty, flamboyant air to a patterned one. Cushions in contrasting fabric spell comfort.

A throw-over sofa cover is easy on the eye, the purse and one's sewing skills (above). Any fabric that drapes well and falls into soft folds is suitable. Sewing can be kept to a minimum. Here, the material covering the sofa arms is folded into wide pleats which are then stitched flat, down the centre, to keep them in place.

DIVAN COVER AND VALANCE

For divan cover:
fabric (we used ticking)
piping cord
thread
zipper (length of one long side of divan)

Measure the length and width of the mattress and add 1.5cm seam allowance on all edges, for top and bottom cover pieces. Measure depth and circumference of mattress and add 1.5cm seam allowance on all edges, for wall piece.

Cut one fabric piece for top cover and one for bottom cover. Trim the corners of each cover piece into a curve. Cut and join fabric strips for wall piece.

Piping will be stitched around three sides (two short sides and one long side) of bottom cover piece, and around four sides of top cover piece. Measure around cover and make required amount of piping following instructions on page 125.

Stitch piping around all sides of top cover piece. Stitch piping around three sides of bottom cover piece, continuing piping around the corners of the remaining side.

Stitch wall pieces together to give a continuous loop. Pin and stitch one edge of wall around three piped sides of bottom cover piece. Insert zipper between edge of wall and unpiped edge of bottom cover following instructions on page 126. Open zipper.

Pin and stitch other edge of wall around top cover piece. Clip seam allowance at corners and neaten seams. Turn right side out, insert mattress and close zipper.

For valance:
fabric (we used ticking)
thread

Measure the width and length of divan base and add 1.5cm seam allowance on all edges, for base panel. Measure circumference of divan base, double the measurement and add 1.5cm seam allowance, for skirt length. Measure from divan base to desired depth and add 1.5cm seam allowance on all edges, for skirt depth.

Cut one fabric piece for base panel. Cut and join fabric strips for skirt piece. Trim the corners of base panel into a curve.

If desired, skirt may be made to fit around three sides of divan rather than four.

Join ends of skirt pieces to give a continuous loop. Neaten and stitch a narrow hem on one edge of skirt piece. Stitch two rows of gathering along other edge of skirt. Pull up gathers to fit around base panel. Pin skirt around base panel, concentrating extra gathers at each corner. Stitch and neaten seam and place valance over divan base.

Square Cushion and Plain Bolster instructions on page 28.

FURNITURE COVERS/62

RE-COVERING A CHAIR WITH UPHOLSTERED SEAT

upholstery fabric
calico (for underneath seat)
wadding
strong thread
upholstery needle
small tacks
upholstery tacks
dressmaker's chalk

Measure the seat and sides and add 8cm on all edges, for seat piece. Measure underneath seat and add 2cm allowance on all edges, for lining under seat. Cut one seat piece from upholstery fabric. Cut one lining piece from calico.

Remove old cover from seat. If there is a thin layer of wadding, remove this too. Trim new wadding to fit seat, place on seat and secure with large tacking stitches. Mark centre of fabric and chair with chalk and place new cover fabric on seat, matching centres.

Fix fabric to seat frame with a few evenly spaced upholstery tacks at each side of the chair (diagram 1).

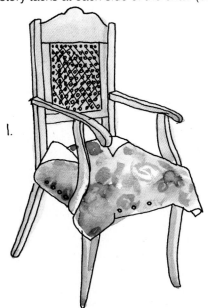

Fold over corner of fabric next to back uprights to right side. Clip fabric from the corner to the fold (diagram 2).

Fold fabric around upright, trim excess fabric from corners, leaving 2cm allowance for turn-under. Fold allowance under and tack fabric to frame next to chair legs. Clip fabric to fit around uprights in similar fashion.

Fold the excess fabric at front corners into a pleat, making sure foldline falls at the corner edge of chair (diagram 3). Adjust tacks if necessary to give a smooth even finish, add extra tacks if required.

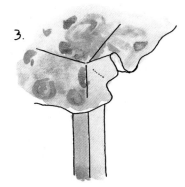

Pull fabric around bottom edge of seat frame, tack in place under the frame using small tacks, trim excess. Fold 2cm allowance under all around calico. Tack calico in place under seat, over raw edges of cover fabric. Clip and trim fabric around legs as for uprights.

If seat is deep, slip-stitch the fold of the front corner pleat in place using upholstery needle and strong thread.

OPTIONAL FINISH. If chair has a decorative seat frame, fabric can be tacked at top edge of frame and trimmed below tacks. Braid can be glued over raw edge to give a neat finish. Fold under 1cm on one end of braid and place a tack inside the fold. Tack braid end over fabric edge (diagram 4), glue braid in place around frame securing with another tack, as before, at the other end.

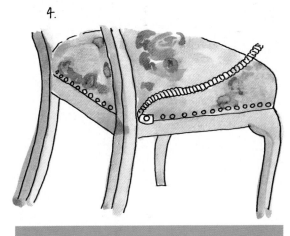

Fabric: Cushion and Director's Chair: Whitehouse Interior Design

TABLE LINEN

Dress up a table with a frilled, flounced or scalloped edged cloth — they're all easily made, yet instantly brighten any setting. We've included instructions for making pretty placemats, embroidered napkins, and how to measure for a perfectly sized cloth. Plus, simple decorating tips; overlay several lace edged cloths, stitch on a tasselled fringing, add a border of grosgrain ribbon or a contrasting binding to transform a simple cloth into a splendid table accessory.

LEFT: Striped Table Set.

STRIPED TABLE SET

RECTANGULAR CLOTH WITH FRILL

1.6m x 115cm-wide plain fabric
1.9m x 150cm-wide striped fabric
thread

Finished size: 250cm x 140cm; cloth fits 150cm x 90cm table.

Cut one 152cm x 92cm plain fabric piece for top of cloth. Cut seven 150cm x 27cm striped fabric strips for frill. 1cm seam allowance is included.

Join frill strips across narrow edges to make a continuous loop. Stitch a narrow hem around one long edge of frill strip.

Stitch two rows of gathering along raw edge. Pull up gathers to fit plain fabric piece.

Pin frill around plain fabric piece, easing the gathers evenly. Stitch and neaten seam.

PLACEMAT AND CUTLERY TIES

For four placemat and four cutlery ties:
30cm x 150cm-wide striped fabric
thread

Finished size: Placemat ties 50cm x 2cm; cutlery ties 40cm x 5cm.

Cut four 50cm x 6cm placemat ties and four 40cm x 12cm cutlery ties. 1cm seam allowance is included.

With right sides of fabric together, fold strips in half lengthways. Stitch across ends diagonally and along raw edge leaving a small opening in seam (see diagram).

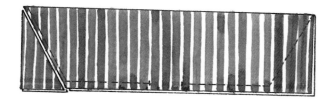

Turn under seam allowance along raw edge of border, press. Fold under corners of fabric allowance to give a "mitred-look" border (diagram 2).

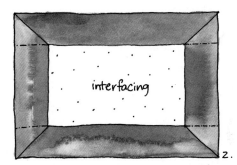

Centre striped fabric piece over interfacing and under border edge. Pin and tack to hold in position. Machine close to folded edges at corners and around inside border, stitching through all layers of fabric (diagram 3).

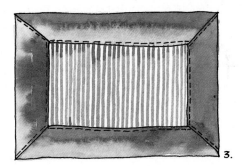

Trim seams, turn right side out. Handstitch openings closed.

STRIPED PLACEMAT

For four tablemats:
90cm x 115cm-wide plain fabric
20cm x 150cm-wide striped fabric
60cm x 90cm-wide fusible interfacing
thread

Finished size: 40cm x 30cm.

Cut 54cm x 44cm plain fabric piece, 30cm x 20cm striped fabric piece and 40cm x 30cm interfacing piece. 1cm seam allowance is included.

Press interfacing to wrong side of plain fabric leaving a 7cm border of fabric around edges. Fold in and press border towards interfaced side of placemat (diagram 1).

NAPKIN WITH FRILL

See page 78 for instructions.

MEASURING FOR TABLECLOTHS

If the diameter or width of your cloth is greater than the fabric width, fabric will have to be joined. This is usually done by joining a strip along each side of the centre piece, avoiding seams in the cloth centre.

SQUARE

Measure across table (a) and add twice the overhang measurement (b). Overhang can be to your lap or to the floor. Include hem allowance in overhang measurement.

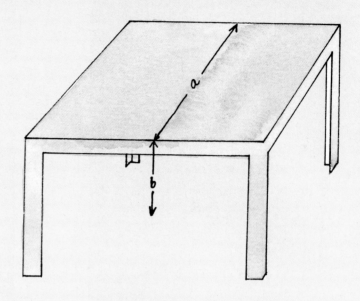

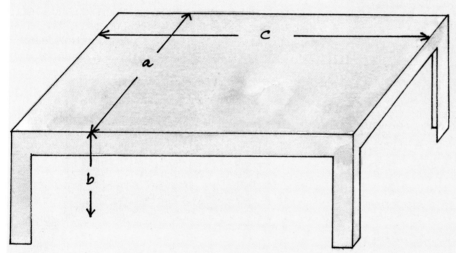

RECTANGULAR

Measure across table (a) and add twice the overhang measurement (b) to calculate width. Measure across table (c) and add twice overhang (b) to calculate length. Include hem allowance in overhang measurement.

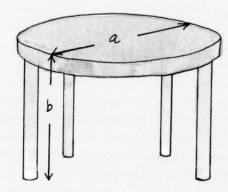

ROUND

Measure diameter of table (a) and add twice the overhang measurement (b). Overhang can be to your lap, to the floor, or longer to drape over the floor. Include hem allowance in overhang measurement.

Fabric: Greenwich by John Kaldor

ROUND CLOTH WITH FRILL

3.6m x 140cm-wide fabric
thread
string
pencil

Finished size: 194cm diameter; cloth fits 73cm high, 48cm diameter table.

Cut one 176cm x 140cm fabric piece and two 176cm x 20cm fabric pieces for cloth. Cut and join 12cm-wide fabric strips for frill to give an 11m frill length (this is approximately twice the circumference of the cloth. 1cm seam allowance is included.

With right sides together, stitch 20cm-wide pieces to each side of 140cm-wide piece along 176cm edges (see diagram 1 Round Cloth with Overlay on next page). Trim and neaten seams, press.

Following instructions for Round Cloth with Overlay (overpage) fold fabric in half lengthways and then widthways. Using a string and pencil, draw a quarter circle with an 88cm radius (see diagram 2 Round Cloth with Overlay below). Cut out cloth.

Stitch the ends of frill strip together to give a continuous loop. Stitch a narrow hem on one edge of frill.

Stitch two rows of gathering along other edge, pull up gathers. Fold the frill and the cloth into quarters and mark these points with a pin.

With right sides together, pin frill to cloth matching pins and easing gathers evenly. Stitch frill to cloth. Trim and neaten seam.

ROUND CLOTH WITH OVERLAY

For cloth:
4m x 120cm-wide fabric (we used chintz)
thread
string
pencil

Finished size: 194cm diameter; cloth fits 73cm high, 48cm diameter table.

Cut fabric into two 2m lengths. Cut one length in half lengthways to give two 60cm-wide lengths. 1cm seam allowance is included.

Stitch one 60cm-wide fabric length to each side of the 120cm-wide length (diagram 1). Neaten and press seams.

Fold fabric in half lengthways and then in half widthways. Tie one end of a string to a pencil and pin the other end to the centre of fabric piece. Adjust string to measure 98cm. Mark a quarter circle with a 98cm radius on fabric (diagram 2).

Cut along pencil line through all layers of fabric.

Neaten raw edge and stitch a 1cm hem around cloth edge, press.

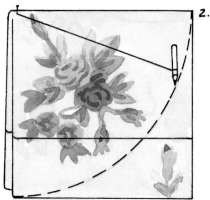

For overlay:
1.1m x 115cm-wide fabric
thread

Finished size: 1m square.

Cut 102cm square fabric piece. 1cm seam allowance is included.

Turn under and press a narrow hem around all edges of fabric. Stitch, press.

CLOTH WITH SCALLOPED EDGE

1.4m x 140cm-wide fabric (we used damask)
thread
water-soluble pen
cardboard
typing paper

Finished size: 138cm square; cloth fits 90cm square table.

Make scalloped cardboard template by drawing semi-circles along the edge of the cardboard, using a glass as a guide. Trim cardboard edge into scalloped pattern.

Using a water-soluble pen, trace scallops along all edges of fabric, positioning top of scallops 1cm from edge of fabric.

Using close zigzag (satin) stitch, stitch along marked line, turning fabric between each scallop.

Using sharp scissors, trim fabric close to stitching (see diagram). Clip between scallops and stitch again, if necessary.

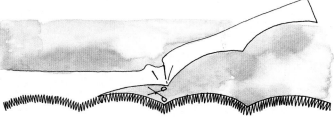

NOTE. If fabric puckers when stitching, place a strip of typing paper underneath fabric. Remove the paper when stitching is complete.

Mixing and matching patterns can produce stunning and subtle effects (left). The stronger the colours used, the bolder the look, as this circular, floor-length cloth topped with a short overlay demonstrates. The scalloped edge detail adds extra interest.

Colour and texture are juxtaposed in a spirited interpretation of the standard flowery tablecloth (right). The shape of the cloth is strongly defined by a dark green grosgrain border, while the edge is embellished with tassels. In place of a corded fabric such as grosgrain, a matt or lustrous trim could be used to create a different effect.

An exercise in shape, pattern and texture combinations (left). Romantic lace forms a happy alliance with full-blown florals. Taking inspiration from the Victorian and Edwardian eras, an ordinary round table is transformed into a charming setting for china and flowers. The full-length, round undercloth is surmounted by a square, white cloth trimmed with handkerchief-points of lace, and then topped by another white square featuring a scalloped lace edging.

The strong pattern on this floor-length tablecloth is crisply accented by a plain, bound edging (right). This could either echo one of the colours in the cloth or be chosen as a contrast.

Table: Country Form

PLEATED PLACEMAT

50cm x 140cm-wide fabric (for border)
30cm x 140cm-wide contrasting fabric
30cm x 90cm-wide fusible interfacing
thread

Finished size: 30cm x 40cm.

Cut one 50cm x 40cm fabric piece for border. Cut a 40cm x 30cm interfacing piece. 1cm seam allowance is included.

Pleat 140cm x 30cm contrasting fabric to form a 40cm x 30cm piece. Our pleats were about 13mm-wide, but pleats can be wider or narrower to accomodate the pattern on fabric.) Tack panel to hold pleats in place. Trim panel to 35.5cm x 25cm, press panel.

Centre and press interfacing onto wrong side of border piece. Complete as for Striped Placemat on page 67, making 4cm-wide finished border.

NAPKIN WITH BOUND EDGE

40cm square fabric
1.7m x 3cm-wide contrasting bias binding (to make
your own bias, see instructions on page 125)
thread

Finished size: 39cm square.

5mm seam allowance is included.

Trim corners of fabric into curves, using a saucer as a guide.

With right sides facing, pin one edge of bias binding around napkin edge. Stitch bias to napkin, clip corners (see diagram). Overlap ends of bias and turn under 1cm on upper strip to give a neat finish.

Turn under and press 5mm along raw edge of bias. Fold bias in half towards back of napkin. Easing bias around corners, pin binding to napkin. Slip-stitch binding into stitching line.

NAPKIN WITH FRILL

32cm square plain fabric
20cm x 150cm-wide striped fabric
thread

Finished size: 42cm square.

Cut and join striped fabric to give a 225cm x 8cm fabric strip for frill. 1cm seam allowance is included.

Join frill strip at narrow ends. Stitch a narrow hem around one long edge of frill strip.

Stitch two rows of gathering around raw edge. Pull up gathers to fit around plain fabric piece. Pin frill to plain fabric, easing gathers evenly.

Stitch and neaten seam.

NAPKIN WITH SCALLOPED EDGE

40cm square fabric (we used damask)
thread
water-soluble pen or dressmaker's pencil
cardboard

Finished size: 38cm square.

Make as for Cloth with Scalloped Edge on page 73.

NAPKIN WITH TEACUP APPLIQUE

40cm square linen
scrap of linen, extra
water-soluble pen or dressmaker's pencil
six stranded embroidery thread, in white

Finished size: 39cm square.

Turn under and stitch a narrow hem around all edges of linen. Turn under again and topstitch around edges.

Trace actual size pattern pieces (see diagram) and transfer to linen scrap using a water-soluble pen or dressmaker's pencil. Work eyelets, star stitches and backstitches on cup and saucer, in one strand of white thread, before cutting out pieces. See page 126 for stitch instructions.

Cut out pattern pieces adding 5mm allowance around each piece. Turn under, clip and press edges around cup and saucer pieces. Pin and tack cup and saucer pieces to napkin corner, slip-stitch in place.

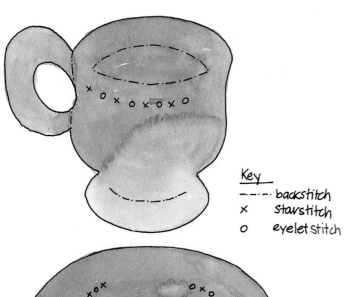

Key
- - - - backstitch
× starstitch
o eyelet stitch

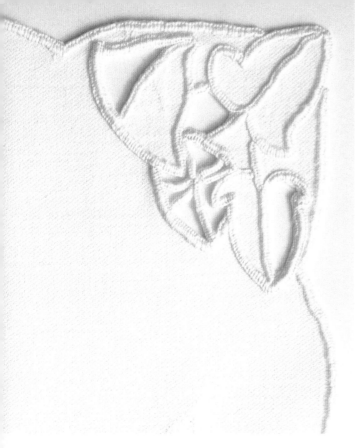

NAPKIN WITH CUTWORK

37cm square fabric (we used damask)
six stranded embroidery thread, in white
water-soluble pen or dressmaker's pencil
cardboard

Finished size: 35cm square.

Make scalloped cardboard template by drawing semi-circles along the edge of cardboard, using a glass as a guide. Trim cardboard edge into scalloped pattern.

Using a water-soluble pen and cardboard template, trace scallops along all edges of fabric, positioning top of scallops 1cm from fabric edge. Using three strands of embroidery thread work scalloped line in buttonhole stitch. See page 126 for stitch instructions. When scalloped line is complete, carefully trim fabric next to stitching, using sharp scissors.

Trace cutwork design (see actual size diagram) and transfer to corner of napkin using water-soluble pen or dressmaker's pencil. Using three strands of embroidery thread work design in buttonhole-stitch. When embroidery is complete, cut away shaded areas carefully, using sharp scissors.

For buttonhole stitch bar, where fabric on both sides of

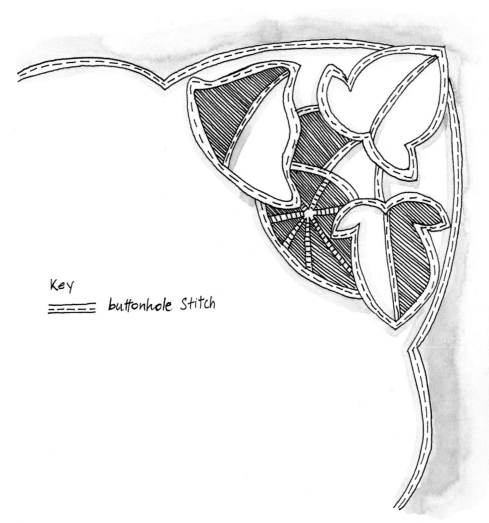

Key
===== buttonhole Stitch

stitching is cut away, work two rows of running stitch along the bar before cutting out fabric. Work buttonhole stitch as marked on diagram, making stitches surround the fabric bar.

NAPKIN WITH BLUE EMBROIDERY

40cm square linen
six stranded embroidery thread, in three shades of blue (we used DMC 792, 797 and 322)
water-soluble pen or dressmaker's pencil

Finished size: 38cm square.

5mm seam allowance is included.

Turn under and stitch a narrow hem around all edges of linen. Turn under again and topstitch around edges.

Trace design (see actual size diagram) and transfer to napkin corner using water-soluble pen or dressmaker's pencil.

Using a single strand of embroidery thread, fill leaves with satin stitch and work outlines in stem stitch. Work fine stems in stem stitch. Use colours as desired. See page 126 for stitch instructions.

Fabric: Les Olivades

LAMPSHADES

Table lamps are meant to be seen so their design is as important as the light they produce; choose a lampshade and base that suit the style and size of the room. Pleated paper and cut paper shades are relatively inexpensive, easy to make and look wonderful in almost any room while fabric lampshades can be made to match curtains, sofas or other fabrics which feature in a room.

Bear in mind that light can be affected by the colour and texture of the lampshade. Pale pink, peach or cream colours produce a rosy glow while very dark colours block out light except where the light escapes through the top and bottom of the shade. Experiment with materials over a lit lampshade to see the effect.

LEFT: Bonded Lampshade.

To make a pattern for cover, place frame on paper and mark the position of one strut and top and bottom ring. Also make a pencil mark on the first strut. Carefully roll the frame, drawing positions of top and bottom rings, until you have a complete outline of frame (diagram 1).

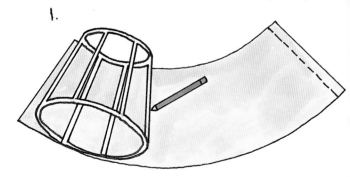

1.

Add 1cm overlap on one straight edge of pattern. Cut out pattern. Position pattern around frame and check accuracy.

Cut out pattern in cardboard.

Spray glue cardboard to wrong side of fabric, positioning cardboard to suit fabric pattern. Cut fabric around cardboard, adding 1cm allowance on one straight edge.

Fold 1cm allowance to wrong side, glue in place.

Fold bias tape in half lengthways over top lampshade ring. Glue tape onto ring, clip tape at struts (diagram 2). Repeat to cover bottom ring.

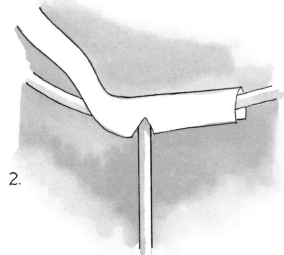

2.

Cut a 4cm-wide bias strip of fabric. Fold in half lengthways and glue over tape-covered top ring, overlapping ends of bias.

Apply glue to top and bottom rings. Place fabric covered cardboard around frame, glue edge with turned fabric allowance over raw edge. Hold in place with pegs until glue dries.

Trim any excess or uneven edges of cardboard at top and bottom of frame. To finish top and bottom edges, glue a bias strip or braid in place.

BONDED LAMPSHADE

fabric
lampshade frame (we used tapered drum frame)
bias cotton lampshade tape
craft glue
spray adhesive
thin cardboard
pencil
paper
pegs

Lamp base: Home and Garden

CUT PAPER LAMPSHADE

lampshade frame (we used a tapered drum shape)
heavy paper
paper (for pattern)
pencil
craft glue
craft knife or scalpel
adhesive tape

Draw a paper pattern following instructions for Bonded Lampshade on page opposite. Add 1cm for overlap along one straight edge of pattern. Add 5mm to top edge of pattern, and 3cm to bottom edge of pattern.

Mark a scalloped line around bottom edge of pattern, using a glass as a guide to draw the semicircles, and beginning and ending at deepest point of scallop. Cut out paper pattern.

Tape pattern onto heavy paper, cut around pattern.

Draw cut-out design (see diagram) on paper in desired positions. Using a craft knife, cut along each line being careful not to cut out any paper pieces.

actual size

Position paper around frame, check fit, trim if necessary. Run a line of glue along top and bottom ring of frame and along one straight edge of paper. Place paper around frame, trim end scallop if necessary.

GATHERED LAMPSHADE

fabric
lampshade frame (we used a tapered drum shape)
6mm-wide elastic

This cover is held under the bottom ring of the frame by elastic in the bottom edge casing, at the top it is stitched to the ring.

Cut one piece fabric 1½ times circumference of bottom ring x frame height plus 10.5cm, for cover. Cut one 114cm x 3.5cm piece fabric for large tie. Cut six 10cm x 1.5cm pieces fabric for small ties.

With right sides together, stitch short edges of cover piece together. Press under 5mm along each long edge, then press under 1.5cm for casing on lower edge and 3.5cm for casing on top edge.

Stitch next to both folded edges of lower casing leaving a small opening to insert elastic.

Stitch top casing next to lower folded edge. Stitch another line 2cm above this stitching.

Clip a small hole in top edge casing at centre front of cover. Handstitch over the raw edges of hole to make an eyelet.

Fold large tie piece in half lengthways, right sides together and stitch along 114cm edge. Turn right side out, trim ends diagonally and fold in raw edges. Stitch across ends. Press and thread tie through eyelet in top casing.

Stitch the six small ties in same way as large tie.

Place lampshade cover over frame. Pull up large tie and tie ends into a bow; tie should sit just under the top ring. Stitch the six ties around inside top edge of cover, placing them 2cm below the top edge and evenly spaced. Knot each tie onto top ring.

Whip-stitch top casing to top ring along upper stitching line of casing. Insert elastic through bottom casing. Pull up elastic in bottom casing to fit under the bottom ring. Stitch elastic ends together and handstitch opening closed. Distribute gathers evenly.

Wooden book stack: Home and Garden

PLEATED PAPER LAMPSHADE

wallpaper (sized) or heavy paper
cord
strong thread
1cm-wide cotton tape
lampshade frame (we used tapered drum frame)
craft glue
leather punch

Cut wallpaper rectangle twice the circumference of the bottom ring of the frame x height of the shade plus 5cm (this allows the cover to extend 2cm over the top edge and 3cm over the bottom edge).

Wrap tape around the top and bottom rings of the frame (diagram 1), stitch ends together.

On the wrong side of the paper, lightly draw lines 4cm apart across the width. Mark a dot halfway between each line. Fold along the first line using a ruler to give a neat crease, make sure fold is at right angles to paper edge.

Make the next crease at the dot between the lines, changing the direction of the pleat so they will be "concertina fashion". Continue making 2cm-wide pleats along the paper (diagram 2).

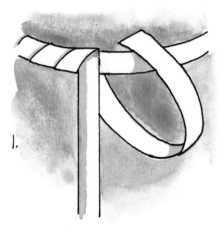

Punch a hole in the centre of each pleat, 2cm in from top edge. Repeat along bottom edge punching holes 3cm in from bottom edge.

Overlap and glue the ends of pleated cover neatly together so that one end sits inside a finished pleat. Allow the glue to dry before continuing. Thread the cord through the top edge holes and pull up to fit the top ring. Stitch cord ends together securely. Repeat for bottom edge.

Using double thread, attach the top edge cord to the frame by whipping over the cord between each pleat and over the ring (diagram 3). Keeping the thread taut, work all around the ring and fasten off by stitching thread to the tape. Make sure the pleats are placed evenly. Attach the lower edge to the bottom ring in the same way.

Lamp base: Home and Garden. Stationery: Kenny's Cardiology

WINDOW DRESSING

Window treatments offer privacy, insulation from noise and temperature, and protection from harsh light, as well as being decorative features. They can also enhance, or hide, both the window and the outdoor scene.

Choose a functional fabric and style which suits the room; a heavy tapestry drape for a lavish dining setting, a coloured canvas blind for a bright, busy kitchen, a filmy white lace curtain for a romantic bedroom or vivid chintz drawn into a frilled Austrian blind for a comfortable sitting room. Seek professional advice when selecting from the myriad of heading tapes, blind cords, curtain linings, tracks and poles, and always be prepared to experiment with non-furnishing fabrics for an individual look.

LEFT: Curtain with Gathered Heading.
Tie-back hook: Home and Garden

MEASURING UP

To estimate the finished width of curtains, measure the width of the rod or track (if it is curved and sits out from the wall include the extra distance around the curves). For most heading styles, multiply the finished width by two to allow for fullness in mediumweight or heavyweight fabrics and triple the width for sheer or lightweight fabrics (this will vary with different headings).

It may be necessary to join fabric widths to achieve the desired fullness. Work out how many widths of fabric are required by dividing the width of the curtain by the width of the fabric. Calculate the number of panels you will need, being careful to allow extra fabric when matching patterns.

To estimate the finished length of a curtain, measure from the top of the rod or track to where the curtain will fall (see diagram). This will vary depending on whether the curtain falls to the sill or floor (a); is fitted into the window recess (b) or runs from halfway down the window to sill, as in cafe curtains.

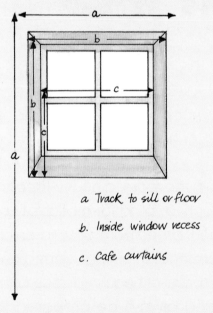

a Track to sill or floor

b. Inside window recess

c. Cafe curtains

Add hem and heading allowances for each fabric length (these will vary according to the type of heading tape and whether it is to be hung from above or below the track). If falling to the floor, allow 1cm less so the fabric clears the floor.

To estimate the overall fabric required for curtains, multiply the length of each fabric piece by the number of widths required.

TRACKS AND POLES

Like heading tapes, these come in a variety of styles ranging from flexible tracks to decorative wooden poles. Most tracks come in metal and plastic and can be bought in a range of colours.

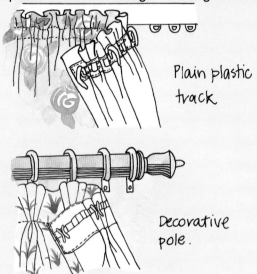

Plain plastic track

Decorative pole.

Choose a simple track if a pelmet is to be fitted, as it will be concealed. For a wall-fitted track the curtains can conceal the track, if desired, or hang below the track depending on the type of heading chosen.

WEIGHTS

Weights are used to give shape and hold lower edges of curtains in place. The major choice of weights is between a continuous string, or weight tape, which is slipped into the bottom hem or large circular weights which are stitched to the curtain corners. The string of weights is used for sheer or lightweight fabrics while the individual weights are used in heavier fabrics. When weighting unlined curtains, cover the weight before sewing it to the corner of the hem. In lined curtains the lining should hang over the weight.

HEADING TAPES

These come in a variety of styles and have superseded time-consuming hand-worked headings. Tapes can form gathers, pinch pleats, pencil pleats and many other styles. Choose the style of heading tape before buying fabric as it will influence the amount of fabric required.

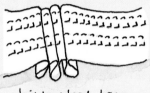

standard tape

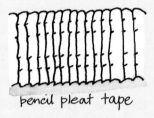

triple pleat tape.

pencil pleat tape

Tapes have cords which are pulled up to form pleats or gathers, or slots to insert pronged hooks which pleat the fabric. They are available in a variety of widths and weights to suit the fabric and style of the curtains. Heading tape is usually attached a couple of centimetres below the top of the curtain to give the heading shape and stiffness.

Cut heading tape 3cm longer than fabric width. Knot cords at one end of tape on wrong side of tape. Turn under a hem at the raw edges of tape. Pin and stitch tape across top of curtain. Pull up cords to give desired effect and wind cords into a figure-eight, knot and leave uncut to allow for readjustment and laundering.

HOOKS

These are attached to the heading tape and the runners to hang the curtain. Some hooks are also used to create pleats in a curtain or to add stiffness to curtain headings. Hooks are generally metal or plastic and come in a variety of sizes and styles to suit tapes.

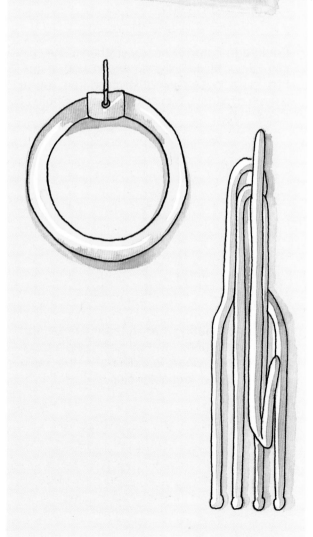

LININGS

Linings give a finished look to curtains, protect fabric from fading in strong light and insulate against heat, cold and noise. Cottons, calico and sateens are most often used for linings; fabrics coated with acrylic and other insulating materials are also available. Linings are usually either loose, locked-in or detachable. It is best to make the lining as full as the curtain, so calculate fabric accordingly.

Loose lining is stitched together with the curtain at the side seams and top, and left free at the bottom edge.

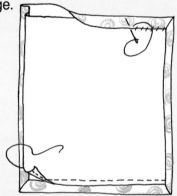

Locked-in lining is loosely stitched to the curtain fabric. Place lining on wrong side of curtain, stitch loose rows of stitching from top to bottom of curtain. Slip-stitch lining to curtain at sides.

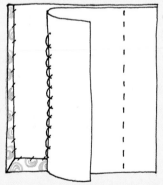

Detachable lining has heading tape and hooks which attach to the main curtain tape. Convenience when laundering is the main advantage of detachable lining.

RUNNERS

The type of runners chosen depends on the style of track. Tracks usually have a particular type of runner to fit each style. These can range from plastic runners which slide along the track, to wooden or brass rings which are used on a decorative pole. Runners often have eyes through which the curtain hooks are attached.

Cafe curtain rings may have clips which expand to hold the curtain or eyes which can be stitched through.

When calculating the amount of runners needed, allow one runner for each 10cm of fabric width and an extra one for each outer end of the curtain.

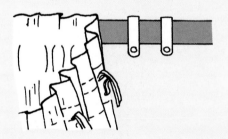

CURTAIN WITH GATHERED HEADING

fabric (lightweight or mediumweight)
gathering tape
thread

NOTE. Gathering tape is the standard and simplest style of heading tape available. The tape gives soft gathers and is most often used on informal and unlined curtains and for small windows. Gathering tape is not suitable for heavy fabrics.

Gathered tape is usually positioned 2cm or 2.5cm from the top edge of the curtain to give a heading. Gathered headings are also used when a pelmet will conceal the curtain top.

For most gathered tapes the fabric should be 2½ times the width of the track plus 5cm for each side hem. For length, add allowance for heading at top of curtain as well as 10cm for bottom hem.

Turn under 2.5cm double hem along each side of curtain, stitch in place.

Turn under and stitch hem at top edge of curtain.

Pin tape over hem at top edge of curtain. Fold under raw ends of tape. Knot cords together at back of tape, on one end of curtain. Stitch tape in position (diagram 1).

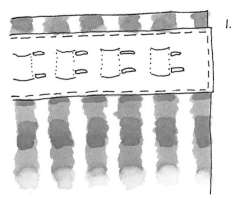

Pull up cords at unknotted end to form pleats. Wind cords into a figure-eight and knot, leaving them uncut (diagram 2).

Turn up and stitch a 10cm hem on bottom edge of curtain.

Fabric: Ascraft

CURTAIN WITH LOOPED HEADING

fabric
thread

To calculate the amount of fabric required, measure the desired width and length. Cut fabric to these measurements adding 1.5cm to top for seam allowance, 2.5cm to each side and 10cm for bottom hem.

Cut facing piece same width as curtain plus 1.5cm for side seams x 12cm. Cut two 16cm x 8cm fabric pieces for each loop.

Place loop pieces right sides together, pin and stitch along 16cm sides. Trim, turn right side out, press.

Fold each loop in half across width. With raw edge of loops and top edge of curtain together, space loops evenly across curtain. Pin and stitch in place.

Stitch side hems on curtain and facing. Turn under and stitch a narrow hem on raw edge of facing.

Place facing and curtain right sides and raw edges together over loops. Pin and stitch (see diagram). Trim seam, turn to right side, press. Stitch across top edge of curtain, stitching through all layers. Slip-stitch facing to curtain at sides. Turn raw edge of curtain under then turn a 9cm-wide hem, stitch in place.

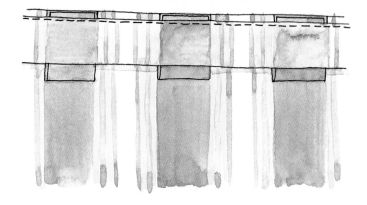

Thread curtain rod through loops.

CURTAIN WITH EYELET HEADING

fabric
fusible interfacing
thread
cord
eyelets

To calculate curtain length, measure from approximately 10cm below curtain rod to length desired. Add 10cm allowance for bottom hem and 1.5cm seam allowance at top. Fabric width should be 1½ times the finished width of curtain plus 5cm allowance on each side for hems.

Cut fabric strip the width of curtain x 11cm, for heading band.

Cut interfacing to same size as band and fuse to wrong side of band. Fold fabric strip in half lengthways, right sides together, stitch across both ends. Trim and turn right side out.

Turn under 2.5cm double hem along each side of curtain and stitch two rows of gathering along top edge. Pull up gathers to fit width of heading band. With right sides together, pin and stitch gathered edge to one long edge of heading band (see diagram). Trim seam, turn right side out. Turn under and press allowance on remaining edge of heading band. Pin and stitch band in place.

Turn up and stitch a 10cm hem on bottom edge of curtain.

Attach purchased eyelets to heading band, spacing them evenly, or have a bootmaker insert eyelets. Thread cord through eyelets and loop cord over pole. Knot cord behind eyelet at each end to finish.

Fabric: Rivtex

Fabric: Les Olivades

CURTAIN WITH PENCIL PLEATS

fabric
pencil pleat tape
thread

NOTE. Pencil pleat tape forms stiff pleats and usually comes with two or three alternative positions for the hooks so they can be adjusted to suit the type of track and the length of the curtain.

For most gathered tapes the fabric should be 2½ times the width of the track plus 5cm for each side hem. For length, add allowance for heading at top of curtain as well as 10cm for bottom hem.

Turn under 2.5cm double hem along each side of curtain, stitch in place.

Turn under and stitch hem at top edge of curtain.

Pin tape over hem at top edge of curtain. Fold under raw ends of tape. Knot cords together at back of tape, on one end of curtain (diagram 1).

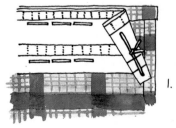

1.

Stitch tape in position. Pull up cords at unknotted end to form pleats (diagram 2).

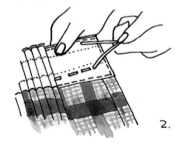

2.

Wind cords into a figure-eight and knot, leaving them uncut (diagram 3).

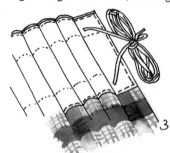

3.

Turn up and stitch a 10cm hem on bottom edge of curtain.

CURTAIN WITH TRIPLE PINCH PLEAT

fabric
pinch pleat tape
thread

NOTE. Pinch pleat tapes either have cords which pull up to form pleats (diagram 1a), or slots to insert pronged hooks which fold the fabric into pleats (diagram 1b).

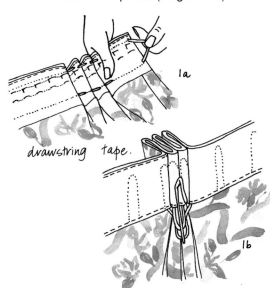

drawstring tape.

slotted tape and pronged hooks

This effect creates formal, stylish curtains which are usually hung from a pole with rings or attached to a track.

Fabric should be 2½ times the width of the pole or track plus 5cm for each side hem. For length, add allowance for heading at top of curtain as well as 10cm for bottom hem.

Turn under 2.5cm double hem along each side of curtain, stitch in place.

Turn under and stitch hem at top edge of curtain.

Fold under raw ends of tape. Pin tape over top edge hem of curtain.

Knot cords together at back of tape, on one end of curtain (see diagram 1 Curtain with Pencil Pleats on opposite page). Stitch tape in position and complete as for Curtain with Pencil Pleats.

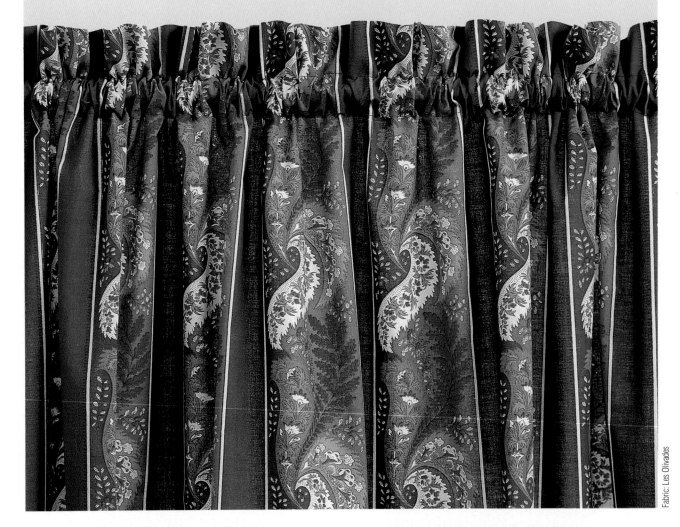

Fabric: Les Olivades

CURTAIN WITH CASING

fabric
thread

Measure curtain length from above the curtain rod at desired height of heading top; add 10cm allowance for heading and casing, and 10cm for bottom hem. Add 5cm for each side hem. Fabric width should be 2 times the width of the pole.

Turn under 2.5cm double hem along each side of curtain, stitch in place.

Turn under 1cm then 9cm on top edge. Stitch hem in place and stitch a second row 4.5cm from the first row, making a casing (see diagram).

Turn up and stitch a 10cm hem on bottom edge of curtain.

CURTAIN WITH SCALLOPED HEADING

fabric
thread
cardboard
water-soluble pen or dressmaker's pencil

NOTE. An inverted scallop heading is usually used for cafe curtains but looks equally as good for long curtains with large curtain rings either sewn or clipped on.

To calculate the amount of fabric required, measure the desired length for curtain from below pole, adding 10cm for the heading and 10cm for bottom hem. Calculate desired curtain width and add 5cm at each side for hems.

Turn under 2.5cm double hem along each side of curtain, stitch in place.

Turn under 5mm then 1cm and stitch a hem on top edge of curtain. With right sides together, fold over 8.5cm at top of curtain, press.

Make a scalloped template by drawing semicircles along the edge of a piece of cardboard; use a teacup as a guide. Our semicircles were 9cm diameter and 2cm apart. Use cardboard template to mark scallops along folded edge of curtain heading.

Stitch along marked lines through both layers of fabric. Trim next to stitching, clip allowance (see diagram). Turn right side out and press.

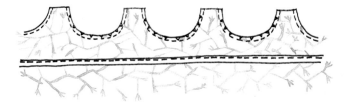

Clip on or stitch rings between each scallop. Turn up and stitch a 10cm hem on bottom edge of curtain.

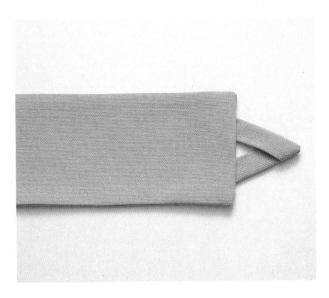

STRAIGHT TIE-BACK

20cm x 120cm-wide fabric
10cm x 90cm-wide fusible interfacing
thread

Finished size: 56cm x 8cm.

Cut two 58cm (or desired length) x 10cm fabric pieces for tie-back. Cut one 58cm x 10cm interfacing piece. Cut two 18cm x 4cm fabric strips for loops. 1cm seam allowance is included.

Press interfacing to wrong side of one tie-back piece. Pin tie-back pieces right sides together. Stitch around three sides, leaving one end open (diagram 1). Trim seam, turn right side out, press. Turn in raw edge on open end and slip-stitch closed.

1.

Turn 5mm on long edges of loop pieces to wrong side. Fold each piece in half lengthways wrong sides together. Topstitch close to folded edges (diagram 2). Fold each loop in half making the fold a 45 degree angle (diagram 3), handstitch fold to secure. Neaten raw ends of loops. Fold loops in half, stitch one to each end of tie-back.

2.

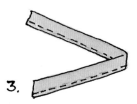

3.

Curtain fabric: Aztec by John Kaldor. Tie-back fabric: Ute by John Kaldor

TIPS FOR TIE-BACKS

The length of tie-backs can be varied to fit your curtains. Measure curtains before cutting fabric and lengthen tie-back pieces as necessary to fit. Heavy fabric creates extra bulk and will require longer tie-backs.

The length of the tie-back loops can also be varied to fit tie-back. When the hooks are small the loops can also be small so 10cm-long pieces will be adequate. For larger ornate hooks adjust loop length to fit.

STENCILLED TIE-BACK

30cm x 120cm-wide fabric
20cm x 90cm-wide fusible interfacing
2 curtain rings
fabric paint
stencil brush
acetate sheet
craft knife or scalpel
thread

Finished size: 58cm x 10cm.

Cut two 60cm (or desired length) x 12cm fabric pieces for tie-back. Cut one 60cm x 12cm interfacing piece. 1cm seam allowance is included.

Press interfacing to wrong side of one tie-back piece. Cut each corner of tie-back piece into a curve (diagram 1). Trim other tie-back piece to match.

1.

Pin tie-back pieces right sides together. Stitch all around leaving a 10cm opening, in the same way as Shaped Tie-Back on page 106. Trim seam, turn right side out, slip-stitch opening closed, press.

Trace stencil design (diagram 2) onto acetate. Cut out design using a craft knife. Position design as desired on tie-back. Dab paint-loaded brush onto cut-out areas of stencil. Repeat design as desired. Allow paint to dry.

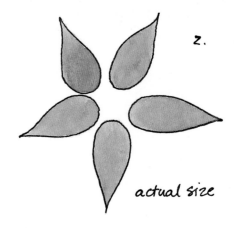

z.

actual size

Stitch a curtain ring to each end of tie-back.

Above left and above right: Tie-back hooks: Home and Garden

Curtain fabric: Sasha by John Kaldor. Tie-back fabric: Simone by John Kaldor

TIE-BACK WITH BOW

40cm x 120cm-wide fabric
10cm x 90cm-wide fusible interfacing
thread

Finished size: 58cm x 8cm.

Cut two 60cm (or desired length) x 10cm fabric pieces for tie-back. Cut two 120cm x 9cm fabric pieces for bow and two 16cm x 5cm fabric strips for loops. Also cut a 60cm x 10cm interfacing piece. 1cm seam allowance is included.

Make as for Straight Tie-Back on page 102.

Pin bow pieces right sides together. Stitch all around leaving one end open. Trim seam and turn right side out, slip-stitch opening closed.

Fold loop pieces in half lengthways, right sides together. Stitch along length, turn right side out. Turn in raw ends and slip-stitch closed. Fold loops in half, stitch one to each end of tie-back.

Tie bow firmly. Stitch in place on tie-back front, about 20cm from one end (or in desired position).

Fabric: Ascraft

TASSEL FRINGED TIE-BACK

10cm x 120cm-wide fabric
10cm x 90cm-wide fusible interfacing
70cm tassel fringe
40cm narrow cord
thread

Finished size: 58cm x 8cm.

Cut two 60cm (or desired length) x 10cm fabric pieces for tie-back. Cut one 60cm x 10cm interfacing piece. Cut length of cord in half. 1cm seam allowance is included.

Make the same way as Straight Tie-Back on page 102.

Pin fringe to one long edge of tie-back. Trim fringe, leaving 1cm extra at each end. Handstitch fringe in place, stitching ends onto wrong side of tie-back.

Fold each cord piece in half, stitch one length to each end of tie-back.

Above left and above: Tie-back hooks: Home and Garden

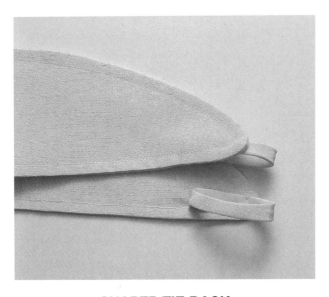

SHAPED TIE-BACK

30cm x 120cm-wide fabric
20cm x 90cm-wide fusible interfacing
thread

Finished size: 58cm x 10cm.

Make pattern following diagram 1.

Cut out fabric and one piece of interfacing using pattern (diagram 1), or increase pattern to desired length. Cut two 16cm x 4cm bias strips for loops. 1cm seam allowance is included.

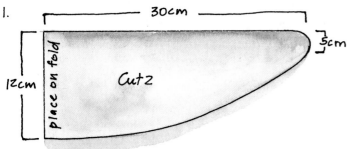

Press interfacing to wrong side of one tie-back piece.

Pin tie-back pieces right sides together. Stitch all around leaving a 10cm opening on the straight edge (diagram 2). Trim seam, turn right side out. Stitch opening closed. Press, topstitch 6mm from edge.

Fabric: Shot Moire by John Kaldor

Fold each loop strip in half lengthways. Stitch along length, trim seam and turn right side out. Turn in raw edges on ends and slip-stitch closed.

Fold loops in half, stitch one on each end of tie-back.

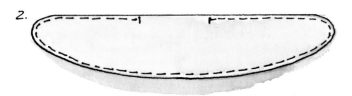

Above and above right : Tie-back hooks: Home and Garden

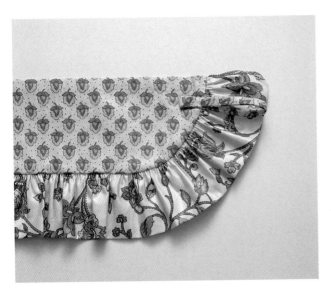

FRILLED TIE-BACK

30cm x 120cm-wide fabric
20cm x 120cm-wide contrasting fabric (for frill)
20cm x 90cm-wide fusible interfacing
thread

Finished size: 58cm x 16cm.

Cut two 60cm (or desired length) x 12cm fabric pieces for tie-back. Cut one 120cm x 14cm contrasting fabric piece for frill. Cut two 20cm x 4cm bias strips for loops. Cut one 60cm x 12cm interfacing piece. 1cm seam allowance is included.

Press interfacing to wrong side of one tie-back piece. Trim a corner on each end into a curve (diagram 1). Trim the other tie-back piece to match.

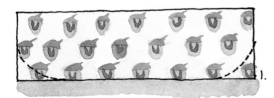

Fold the frill in half lengthways, right sides together. Stitch across ends, trim seam and turn right side out. Stitch two rows of gathering along raw edge of frill.

Pull up gathers to fit the curved edge of the tie-back. Pin and tack frill to interfaced tie-back piece, right sides together (diagram 2). Evenly space gathers.

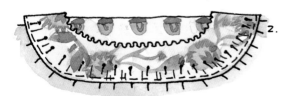

Pin other tie-back piece over frill, right sides of tie-back pieces together. Stitch all around leaving a 10cm open-

Curtain and Tie-back fabrics: Boronia Collection by John Kaldor

ing on the straight edge (diagram 3). Trim seam, turn right side out. Press and stitch opening closed.

Fold loop strips in half lengthways. Stitch along length, trim and turn right side out. Turn in raw edges on ends and slip-stitch closed.

Fold loops in half, stitch one on each end of tie-back.

Short and sweet, this triple-pinch-pleated "frieze" is comprised of separate, short strips of curtain linked by large bows (above). The importance of the bows is emphasised by the use of a bold fabric design that contrasts with the curtains.

A plain binding in a contrasting colour lends definition to a densely patterned fabric (below). A useful device for full-length curtains, it adds a touch of formality. The curtain is pleated at the top and attached to rings on a rod.

Exploit the film-star qualities of slinky, slippery fabric when a dramatic effect is required (above). These deliberately over-long drapes fall in a generous swag are wrapped into a knot and then allowed to fall in glossy profusion to the floor. The curtains are hooked in place against the window frame, the attachment concealed by the knot.

The clean lines of this sublime window treatment hint at sailing away into the deep-blue yonder (left). The filmy, flat curtain is simply hitched up at one corner, then folded back on itself and secured by a hook attached to the window frame.

Use a double layer of sheer fabric to make a theatrical statement. The bottom layer falls straight against the window while the top layer is caught into a soft knot (right). The heading is decorated with a row of neat, contrasting bows.

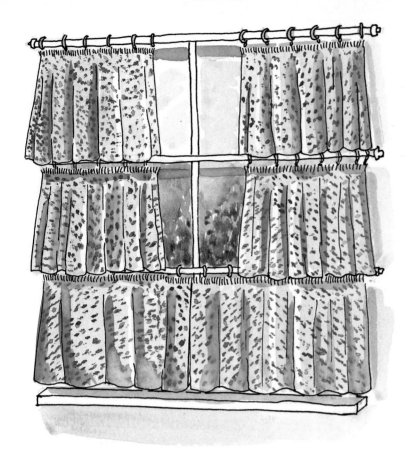

When something unashamedly pretty is called for, in a child's room or bedroom for example, "wedding-cake" tiered curtains are most appropriate (left). Be generous with the amount of material you use; the fullness of each layer is an intrinsic part of the design's appeal. Fabric such as good-quality cotton will hang well and look fresh and crisp. These curtains have gathered headings that are attached to the rings on each of the three poles, making them easy to draw.

Accentuate the shape and proportions of French doors with a pared-down treatment (right). Diaphanous fabric is held flat against the doors by rods, top and bottom. To accentuate the simplicity of the design, each curtain is then encircled by a ribbon tied in a bow at the front. A gauzy curtain fabric will allow the full circumference of the ribbon to be just visible.

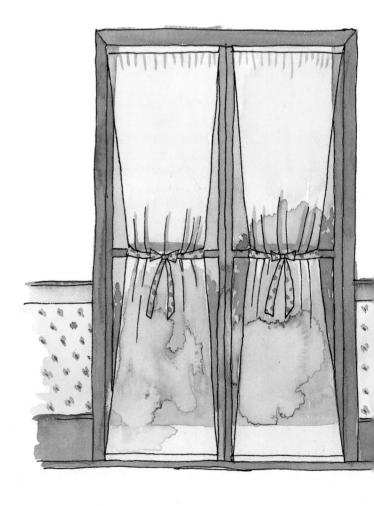

ROMAN BLIND

fabric
lining fabric (same amount as for blind fabric)
Roman blind tape
screw eyes
fine polyester cord
5cm x 2.5cm batten (for heading)
4cm-wide flat batten, width of finished blind (for casing)
staple gun or tacks
cleat
thread

To calculate fabric requirements, measure desired width and add 3cm at each side; measure desired length and add 6cm for top hem and 8cm for bottom hem.

Cut lining piece same length as blind fabric, and 4cm narrower on each side. Mark the centres at top of fabric and lining pieces.

With right sides together, match centres of blind and lining. Pin, tack and stitch along the sides and bottom edge leaving 1cm seam allowance. Trim seams, turn right side out (diagram 1). Press; side seams should fall on lined side of blind.

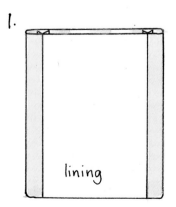

Cut a piece of tape same length as blind. Pin tape from bottom edge, along one side hem, to within 1.5cm of top edge of blind and positioning tape 1.5cm in from sides. Position other lengths of tape parallel to the first tape and evenly spaced across blind (ours were about 40cm apart). Ensure rings on tapes line up horizontally across all rows. Stitch tape in position (diagram 2).

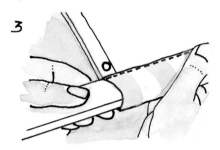

Rings should line up across the blind

Turn up 8cm at base of blind and stitch along upper edge to form batten casing. Insert flat batten (diagram 3) and handstitch casing edges together.

Turn under 1cm allowance on blind and lining fabric along top edge, stitch. If desired, topstitch top edge of blind 10cm from turned-in edge.

Tack or staple fabric to top of heading batten, close to the back edge (diagram 4). If necessary, adjust the position of the fabric on the heading board, so the blind fits the window exactly.

Insert screw eyes into the underside of the wooden heading board so they line up with the rows of tape (diagram 5).

top of blind, through screw eyes in heading batten and to one side. Knot ends of cords together (diagram 6).

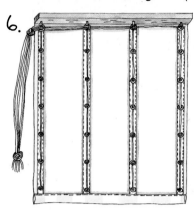

Cut lengths of cord to fit the length of the blind, across the top and down one side of the blind. Knot the first length of cord to the bottom ring on one side length of tape. Thread cord through all rings on this row of tape. Repeat for other lengths of cord. Thread cords across

Mount the batten at the top of the window and attach a cleat to one side of window. Pull up blind and wind the ends of cord around the cleat.

Fabric: Rivtex

LEFT: Roman Blind.
ABOVE: Roller Blind with Cut-Outs.
Above: Table: Country Form. Baskets and box: Corso de Fiori

ROLLER BLIND WITH CUT-OUTS

fabric
fusible blind backing
thread
roller and blind fittings
3cm-wide batten (for lower edge)
staple gun or tacks (if using wooden roller)

To calculate fabric requirements, measure window, sub-tract 1.5cm (or less, as desired) at each side for roller fittings and add 3cm to each side for hem. Measure desired length, add 5cm for bottom casing and 30cm for top allowance around roller.

Cut backing fabric to finished size of blind (not includ-ing hem and casing allowances), making sure edges are straight and parallel. Use a set square to cut corner right angles accurately.

Mark the centres of fabric and backing. Place the wrong side of the fabric over the fusible side of the back-ing, matching centres and leaving the 3cm allowance free on both sides.

Bond fabric to backing following manufacturer's direc-tions. Press using high temperature, from centre of fabric to edges, and from fabric side rather than backing side. Leave blind to cool before moving, to allow fabrics to bond securely.

Press 3cm in along both sides. Stitch 2cm in from folded edge (we used zigzag), trim excess fabric.

If using a metal roller which has a groove to take plastic insertion, stitch top edge of blind to flat edge of plastic strip (diagram 1). If using a wooden roller, neaten top edge of blind.

1.

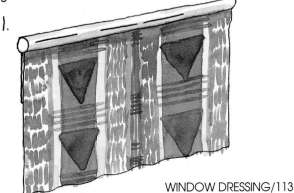

Turn in 1cm then 4cm on lower edge of blind for casing and stitch next to edge (diagram 2).

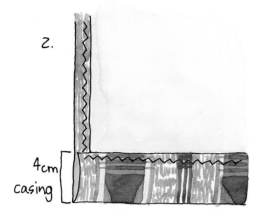

For cut-outs, mark position and shape, as desired. Zigzag around marked line and cut out fabric inside line.

Insert batten into lower edge of blind.

If using a metal roller, insert plastic strip into groove in roller. If using wooden roller, tack or staple top edge of blind to roller.

Attach fittings to wall and mount blind.

CLOUD SHADE

sheer fabric
heading tape (we used pencil pleat tape)
15mm-wide gathering tape
1cm-diameter plastic rings
fine polyester cord
5cm x 2.5cm batten *or* Austrian blind track
curtain hooks (if using Austrian blind track)
tacks *or* hook and loop tape (if using batten)
cleat
screw eyes
thread

NOTE. The Cloud Shade is made from sheer fabric and has a 70cm bottom section which remains permanently gathered. Gathering tape is stitched onto this section, cords pulled up and tied. Above the gathered section, rings are stitched in line with the tape. These rings hold the cords which allow the blind to be pulled up and down, but remain invisible from the right side of the blind.

To calculate fabric requirements, allow 2½ times the width of the window, plus 5cm for each side hem. Length should be 1½ times the height of the window plus 5cm allowance for heading and 4cm allowance for bottom hem.

Stitch fabric lengths together using fine French seams (see general instructions on page 127).

Turn in and stitch 2.5cm double hem along each side. Turn under 5cm along top edge. Stitch heading tape over this hem on wrong side, following instructions for Curtain with Pencil Pleats on page 98.

Turn up and stitch a 2cm double hem along bottom edge of shade.

At one side, pin a 70cm length of tape from bottom edge of blind along side hem. Position other 70cm lengths of tape parallel to the first tape and evenly spaced across blind (ours were about 40cm apart).

Turn under raw edges of tape and stitch in position.

Stitch rings onto blind, at 10cm intervals, in rows from top of tape to top of blind (diagram 1). Ensure rings line up across blind.

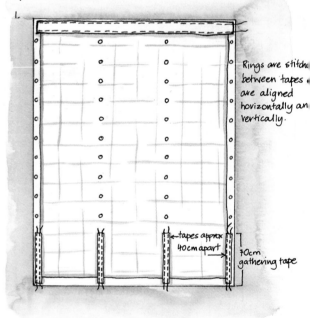

Stitch a ring into the bottom of each tape (along bottom edge of blind). Tie a length of fine cord to this ring and thread cord up through rings allowing enough length to carry it across top of blind and down one side. Repeat for each length of tape.

Pull up cords in gathering tape, knot to secure. Pull up cords in heading tape, knot to secure. Slip curtain hooks into heading tape if using an Austrian blind track.

If using a batten, fix it in position above window. Attach blind to batten with tacks, or hook and loop tape. Fix a screw eye to the batten directly above each top ring in blind. Thread cords through screw eyes and across top of blind to one side (diagram 2).

Above right: Table: Country Form

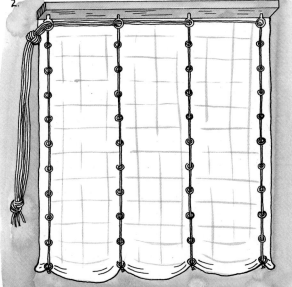

Attach a cleat to the side of the window where the cords are to be secured. Pull cords up and secure around cleat when desired gathered look is achieved. Knot cords together at end.

ROLLER BLIND WITH SHAPED EDGE

fabric
fusible blind backing
thread
roller and blind fittings
3cm-wide batten (for lower edge)
staple gun or tacks (if using wooden roller)

To calculate fabric requirements, measure window, subtract 1.5cm (or less, as desired) at each side for roller fittings and add 3cm to each side for hem. Measure desired length (to bottom of shaped edge), add 30cm for top allowance around roller and 1.5cm seam allowance at bottom edge. Also allow fabric for facing and casing.

Cut backing fabric to finished size of blind (not including side hem allowances), making sure edges are straight and parallel. Use a set square to cut corner right angles accurately.

Mark the centres of fabric and backing. Place the wrong side of the fabric over the fusible side of the backing, matching centres and leaving 3cm allowance free on both sides.

Bond fabric to backing following manufacturer's directions. Press using high temperature, from centre of fabric to edges and from fabric side rather than backing side. Leave blind to cool before moving, to allow fabrics to bond securely.

Press 3cm in along both sides. Stitch 2cm in from folded edge, trim excess fabric.

If using a metal roller which has a groove to take plastic insertion, stitch top edge of blind to flat edge of plastic strip (see diagram 1, Roller Blind with Cut-Outs on page 113). If using a wooden roller, neaten top edge of blind.

To make a pattern for the shaped edge, take a piece of paper half the width of the finished blind and approximately 15cm-wide. Draw desired curved shape along one long edge of paper (see diagram). Cut out fabric for facing piece, adding 1.5cm seam allowance along all raw edges.

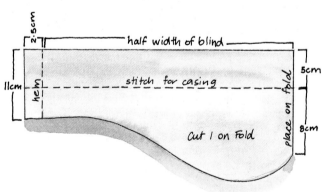

Left: Table and chair: Country Form. Bust: Home and Garden. Boxes and opera glasses: Nouveaux Poor's, Chelsea House Antiques

Place pattern along bottom edge of blind. Cut curved shape along blind edge.

With right sides together, pin facing over lower edge of blind. Stitch along shaped edge, trim and clip curves of seam. Turn facing to wrong side of blind.

AUSTRIAN BLIND

medium-weight fabric
contrasting fabric, for frill (optional)
heading tape (we used pencil pleat tape)
15mm-wide gathering tape
1cm-diameter plastic rings
fine polyester cord
5cm x 2.5cm batten *or* Austrian blind track
curtain hooks (if using Austrian blind track)
tacks *or* hook and loop tape (if using batten)
cleat
screw eyes
thread

NOTE. Our Austrian Blind has a pencil pleated heading and a contrasting frill along the bottom edge.

To calculate fabric requirements, allow 2 times the width of the window, plus 5cm for each side hem. Length should be 2½ times the height of the window plus 5cm allowance for heading. If not attaching a frill, add 4cm allowance for bottom hem.

Stitch fabric lengths together using French seams (see general instructions on page 127).

Turn in and stitch 2.5cm double hem along each side.

Turn under 5cm along top edge.

At one side, pin a length of gathering tape from bottom edge, along side hem, to top edge of blind. Position other lengths of tape parallel to the first tape and evenly spaced across blind (ours were about 40cm apart). Stitch tape in position.

FOR FRILL. Cut a fabric strip twice the width of blind fabric and 20cm-wide. Fold frill strip in half lengthways, wrong sides together, and stitch two rows of gathering along raw edges.

Turn in and slip-stitch ends of frill. Pull up gathers on frill to fit blind. With right sides together, pin and stitch frill to bottom edge of blind, leaving 2cm seam allowance on the blind and 1cm seam allowance on the frill. Trim and neaten frill allowance, leaving blind allowance uncut.

Fold bottom edge blind allowance in half and pin flat, over ends of gathering tape and frill allowance. Stitch blind allowance in place.

Slip rings into tape, ensuring rings line up across blind.

Stitch heading tape along top edge, over ends of gathering tape (see diagram), following instructions for Curtain with Pencil Pleats on page 98.

Fold in 1.5cm at side and top edges of facing. Stitch along long straight edge at top of facing and 3.5cm below first stitching line to form casing. Insert batten into casing. Handstitch edges of facing to blind.

Complete following instructions for Roller Blind with Cut-Outs on page 113.

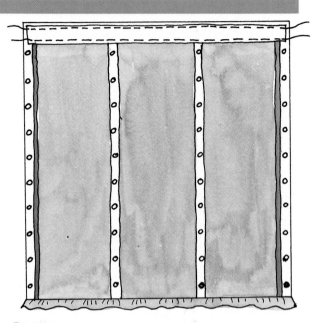

Tie a length of fine cord to each ring at bottom edge of blind and thread cords up through rings. Allow enough length on each cord to carry it across top of blind and down one side.

Fix blind to batten and wall following instructions for Cloud Shade on page 114.

Right: Plants: Michele Shennen's Balmain Garden Centre

BOX PELMET

Construct a support board above the window before taking pelmet measurements. Cut a piece of 2cm thick board so it extends 5cm at each side of the window. Position board 5-10cm above the window and fix with small angle brackets at each end and at regular intervals in between. Nail a square piece of board below and at right angles to each end of the long board, for end pieces.

Measure length of board including end pieces. Decide on depth of pelmet, making sure it covers the support board and keeping in mind the curtain proportions. Cut fabric, lining and heavy interfacing to the required size, adding 1cm seam allowance on all sides.

Trim seam allowance from interfacing, apply interfacing to wrong side of fabric, 1cm in from edges.

Place lining right side together with fabric, stitch all around leaving an opening on one side. Turn right side out, press. Slip-stitch opening closed. Fold each end of fabric to fit board ends and press well to form creases.

Add trimming at this stage, if desired. Apply hook and loop tape to wrong side of pelmet along top edge and along edges of support board, or tack pelmet in place.

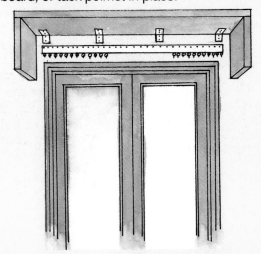

FLAT PELMET

Can be made easily with a straight strip of fabric, interfaced and lined as for Box Pelmet. Make flat pelmet about 20cm wider than window. Attach pelmet to the wall with hook and loop tape or tacks, allowing it to extend 10cm at each side of the window.

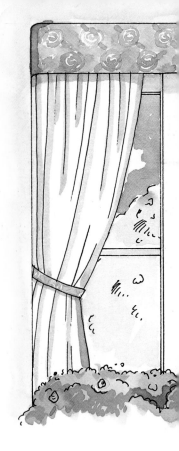

Simple elegance – a box pelmet gives a decorative finish to ordinary curtains (left). Choose a contrasting fabric and coordinate it with tie-backs to give a more formal effect, a stylish contrast or a splash of colour.

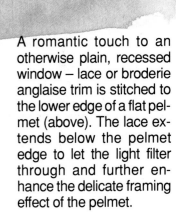

pirited Mexican eometrics form an novative design for at pelmet, enliven- the outlook of a cessed window ft). Sunshine is awn through the ight colours sten- led onto the fabric create a warm and mfortable glow.

A romantic touch to an otherwise plain, recessed window – lace or broderie anglaise trim is stitched to the lower edge of a flat pelmet (above). The lace extends below the pelmet edge to let the light filter through and further enhance the delicate framing effect of the pelmet.

Scallops can softly frame a window, continue the decorative theme of a room or provide a subtle yet dramatic touch (left). Striped, plain or patterned, the flat pelmet can disguise the severe lines of a deep window recess. Variations on this theme could be zigzag edges, square cut-outs or edges cut following the pattern of the pelmet fabric.

GLOSSARY

APPLIQUE: decorative effect created by stitching or gluing fabric pieces onto a fabric background.

BATTEN: length of wood which can be used as a mount for blinds or to weight the bottom edge of a blind.

BIAS BINDING: fabric strip cut at a 45 degree angle to the selvedge and used as a binding. Can be purchased ready made or can be cut from fabric following our instructions on page 125.

BLINDS
AUSTRIAN: blind with gathered heading traditionally made from sheer fabric. It has ringed and corded tapes running vertically down length at regular intervals which create soft ruffled scallops along bottom edge.
BALLOON: similar to Austrian blind. Fabric is gathered by ringed and corded tapes, often has vertical pleats.
CLOUD: similar to Austrian blind and made in sheer fabric, often has a permanently gathered section at the bottom.
FESTOON: similar to Austrian blind. Fabric is gathered vertically into soft ruffles and usually left flat at the heading.
ROLLER: a simple flat blind adjusted in height by means of a roller.
ROMAN: a flat blind with ringed and corded tape running vertically at regular intervals. Scft horizontal folds are formed along bottom edge when blind is raised.

BOLSTER: long cylindrical cushion ideal for use as a sofa armrest or as a head or neck rest.

BONDED FABRIC: two layers of fabric glued wrong sides together to give extra strength, protection or stiffness.

BRACKETS: used to hold curtain rods, blind rollers, tracks or poles out from a wall or window frame. Available in a range of styles for different effects.

BRAID: flat decorative trimming made by braiding lengths of cord together, it can be glued or stitched to fabric.

BROCADE: heavy fabric traditionally woven from cotton or silk and often containing metallic threads. The Jacquard weave gives the fabric a raised pattern.

BUCKRAM: a coarse cotton fabric used for stiffening.

CALICO: lightweight, hard-wearing and washable cotton fabric. Can be purchased unbleached or printed.

CANOPY: fabric draped above and around a bed for decorative purposes.

CANVAS: strong, heavy-duty cotton fabric, ideal for use on outdoor furniture.

CASING: a passage created by folding and stitching a hem through which cord, elastic, ribbon, etc. can be threaded.

CHINTZ: lightweight cotton fabric with a glazed finish, traditionally printed with birds and flowers.

CLEAT: small fixture attached at the side of a window frame and used to secure curtain and blind cords by looping them around the cleat in a figure-eight.

CONTINUOUS CURTAIN FABRIC: curtain fabric which already has a casing and heading.

CURTAIN HEADING: decorative top edge of a curtain, its style affects the fall of the curtain. Most curtain headings are pleated or gathered.

CURTAIN HOOKS: used to attach curtain to track by slotting directly into the heading tape and runners. Different hooks are designed for different effects and to suit different tracks and heading tapes.

CURTAIN LINING: fabric stitched onto the back of a curtain, into the curtain heading, or hung separately behind a curtain to protect curtain fabric from fading, offer extra insulation against light, noise and extreme temperatures, and lend a more tailored look to curtains.

CURTAIN POLE OR ROD: wood, metal or plastic pole or rod from which the curtain is hung. It is supported by brackets fixed to the wall.

CURTAIN RUNNERS: small fixtures which slide freely along a curtain track and to which curtain hooks are attached, enabling curtains to be opened and closed smoothly.

CURTAIN TRACK: a curtain rod with tracks running its length. Curtain tracks are usually sold with runners.

CURTAIN RINGS: rings that are attached to the curtain heading at regular intervals then threaded onto a curtain pole. Curtain is opened and closed by sliding rings along the pole.

CURTAIN WEIGHTS: used in the bottom hem of a curtain to give shape, hold the lower edges in position and prevent curtains from blowing in a breeze. Available in tapes or as individual weights.

CUSHION FILLER: natural or man-made fibres used as stuffing for cushions. Available in loose form such as polyester fibre filling or in foam rubber blocks.

CUSHION INSERT: lightweight fabric casing made to same shape as cushion cover and containing cushion filling. Square and circular inserts can be purchased in standard sizes or inserts can be made to fit non-standard shapes and sizes.

CUTWORK: type of openwork embroidery often used for table linen. A design is stitched onto fabric, then the shapes within a stitched border are cut away.

DAMASK: a Jacquard weave fabric usually made from cotton or linen and traditionally woven with a floral pattern, often used for table linen.

EYELET: small metal ring with hole which is slotted into fabric to create a hole with reinforced edges.

FABRIC FINISHES
FLAME RETARDANT: finishing treatment which prevents or

retards the spread of flames.

MOTH PROOFING: finishing treatment which prevents or discourages insects from eating and ruining fabric.

STAIN RESISTANT: finishing treatment which makes fabric more resistant to water- or oil-based staining. Can be purchased in aerosol form and applied to fabric eg. Scotchgard.

FACING: fabric piece stitched to a raw edge then turned to wrong side to create a neatly finished edge.

FASTENINGS

PRESS STUDS: two small metal or plastic circles designed to fasten when pressed together. They are stitched opposite each other on aligning edges.

HOOK AND EYES: two small metal attachments, one a hook the other either a straight or looped eye, that are stitched opposite each other on aligning edges. Available in different sizes to suit different fabric weights.

HOOK AND LOOP TAPE: consists of two lengths of tape, one with loops, the other with hooks which fasten when pressed together. Used to fasten medium- to heavyweight fabrics. Can be used to attach fabric to a wall: glue one length of tape to the wall, stitch other length to the fabric. Also called touch and close tape. The most common is Velcro.

ZIPPERS: used in soft furnishings where a discreet and neat closure is desired. One side of the zipper is attached to one edge and the other stitched to an aligning edge to join. For instructions on inserting zipper, see page 126.

FINIALS: decorative ends attached to curtain rods or poles.

FLANGE: flat border around a pillowcase or cushion cover, made by stitching at a given distance in from edge or inserting a flat band of fabric into the seam.

FOAM RUBBER FILLING: a firm cushion filler which does not lose its shape. Available in blocks which can be cut to size to fit cushion cover.

FRENCH SEAM: seam where raw edges are enclosed between two lines of stitching, giving a very neat, narrow seam finish. Suitable for sheer fabrics and items where the wrong side will be visible, eg. canopy, cloud blind.

FRINGE: length of trimming consisting of a band of hanging loops, cords or tassels.

FUSIBLE WEBBING: thin, non-woven fabric, usually supported by a layer of paper. The web is saturated with glue which melts when heat and steam are applied. Used to fuse two pieces of fabric together neatly. Useful for applique.

GATHERING: process of pulling up one or more lines of stitching to create soft fabric folds and draw a length of fabric into a given smaller area.

HEADING TAPE: attached across the top of the curtain to create a gathered or pleated effect by drawing up cords or inserting curtain hooks.

INTERFACING: fabric placed between main fabric and facing piece to give extra shape and body. Fusible and non-fusible varieties are available in different weights and degrees of stiffness.

INTERLINING: fabric placed between the curtain and lining to afford insulation against temperature extremes and noise, and add a more tailored look to curtains.

LACE: an openwork and highly decorative fabric made from a wide range of natural and man-made fibres, available in narrow widths for use as a trimming, and in wide fabrics for curtains.

BATTENBURG LACE: (also known as Renaissance lace) made by stitching lengths of lace tape together in a decorative pattern, using needle and thread.

LAMPSHADE FRAMES: metal or plastic-coated metal frames used to support and give shape to a lampshade cover. Available in different shapes and sizes.

LOOSE COVERS: (also called slip covers) removable fabric covers fitted over permanent furniture covers.

MOIRE: a fabric finished with a wavy surface pattern resembling watermarks.

NET: open-weave fabric used for curtains, mosquito nets and canopies.

PELMET: length of stiffened fabric hung from the top of a window to conceal an unsightly curtain track and/or for decorative purposes.

PIPING: length of bias fabric stitched into seams to add a neat, decorative finish. There are two types of piping:

CORDED: bias strip is folded over piping cord.
FLAT: bias strip is folded in half and used without cord.

PLEATS: controlled folds in a fabric piece which create decorative effects and reduce fullness to fit fabric into a given area.

POLYESTER FIBRE FILLING: loose filling of polyester fibre used to stuff cushions.

QUILT: (also known as duvet or doona) bed cover made from two pieces of fabric with a filling such as wadding, feathers or down between. The three layers are then stitched together. Quilting is the process of stitching the fabric layers together.

SCREW EYE: small metal screw with circular hook on one end, often used as a carrier for blind cords.

SHEETING: extra-wide fabric usually used to make bed linen.

SQUAB CUSHION: chair cushion made to fit the seat of a chair and attached to the chair by ties.

STENCIL: a sheet of acetate, paper or bronze etc. with a cut-out pattern. A flat-tipped brush or foam roller is used to apply paint through cut-out areas to produce a pattern.

TACKS: small sharp nails with plain or decorative heads used to attach upholstery to a wooden frame.

TAPESTRY: heavy fabric often woven in a pictorial design and used for cushions and furniture covers. Also a handworked needlepoint picture stitched onto a base fabric.

TARTAN: plaid-like pattern which is traditionally woven into a fabric.

TASSEL: a decorative trim made by wrapping one end of a bunch of cut threads and attaching a hanging loop.

TASSEL FRINGE: length of highly decorative braid with tassels hanging from it at regular intervals.

TEMPLATE: an actual size pattern used to trace around.

TICKING: strong cotton fabric traditionally used to cover pillows and mattresses. Often woven in fine black and white or blue and white stripes.

TIE-BACK: fabric band used to hold a curtain clear of the window.

UPHOLSTERY: padding used to cover furniture. This includes stuffing, springs and covering fabric.

VALANCE: short gathered or pleated skirt fitted around the base of a bed or divan.

WADDING: sheet of thin soft padding available in different thicknesses and used to pad quilts, picture frames, furniture, etc..

GENERAL INSTRUCTIONS

GATHERING

1. Set the machine on the longest stitch length. Stitch two lines of gathering either side of the seamline.

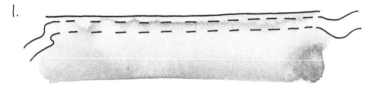

2. Pull up gathering threads until fabric is the desired width. Distribute gathers evenly or as required.

STITCHING A CASING

Fold under raw edge then fold again for casing. Stitch two lines to make the casing. Casing should be at least 5mm wider than the cord or elastic to be threaded.

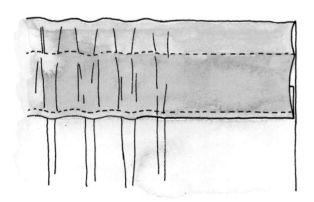

OPEN SEAM

1. Place fabric pieces right sides together. Pin and stitch at desired distance from raw edge. Knot threads at each end or reverse stitch to secure.

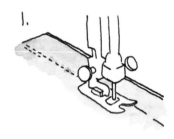

2. Neaten raw edges with zigzag and press open.

CLIPPING AND NOTCHING A CURVED SEAM

A curved seam should be clipped or notched along the seam allowance to ensure it sits flat. Clip an outward curving seam by making small snips in the seam allowance (a), or notch an inward curving seam by cutting small V-shapes out of the seam allowance (b).

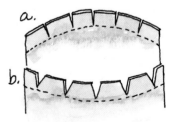

MAKING AND APPLYING BIAS BINDING

1. Fold fabric so lengthwise and crosswise grain align (the bias is at 45 degree angle to the selvedge). Cut bias fabric strips desired width.

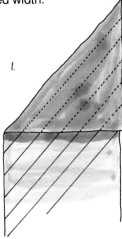

2. Join strips to give desired bias length by stitching across straight grain. Trim next to stitching. If bias is to be used for binding, press a hem on each side of bias strip and press strip in half lengthways.

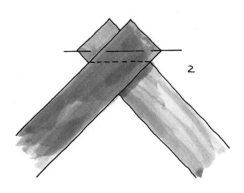

3. To bind fabric edge, align raw edges of bias strip and fabric. Stitch and turn binding over fabric edge. Turn under raw edge of binding and handstitch into stitching line, or (4) machine stitch next to binding edge.

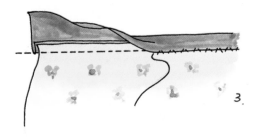

MAKING AND APPLYING CORDED PIPING

1. Fold bias over piping cord. Using a zipper foot, stitch next to cord.

2. Pin piping on fabric, aligning raw edges. Using a zipper foot, stitch in place.

3. Pin remaining fabric piece in position. Stitch seam.

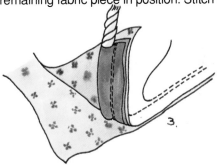

4. To apply piping around corners, clip from raw edge towards stitching. Pin piping around corner, easing to fit.

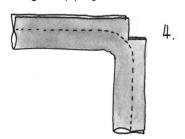

JOINING PIPING

1. To join lengths or ends of piping, fold under one end of the fabric which covers piping. Trim and butt ends of cord. Overlap the folded fabric end over the other end.

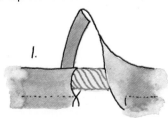

2. Handstitch the fabric ends together.

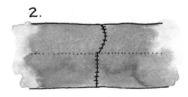

INSERTING A ZIPPER

1. Measure and mark zipper position on the seamline. Tack the seam closed and press seam allowance open.

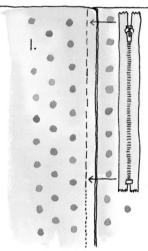

2. Place zipper face down over seam allowance, aligning zipper with seamline. Tack and stitch around the zipper. Unpick all tacking stitches.

BUTTONHOLE STITCH

When working buttonhole stitch for cutwork, stitch a line of running stitch along the outline of the design. Evenly work buttonhole stitches over the running stitch.

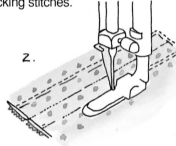

EYELET STITCH

Pierce a small hole with large darning needle. Work close overcast stitches around the raw edge.

STAR STITCH

Work straight stitches into a central point. Stitches can be the same or varied lengths.

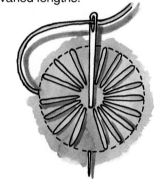

STEM STITCH

BACKSTITCH

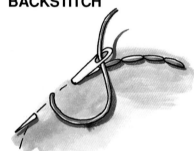

SATIN STITCH

MATCHING PATTERNS

When joining fabric pieces, a more professional finish is achieved by matching the fabric pattern across the seam. To do this, move the pattern pieces up and down, next to each other, until the pattern aligns. The pattern should be matched at the level of the stitching line, rather than the cutting line.

FRENCH SEAM

1. Use a French seam on sheer fabrics or where the wrong side of seam will be visible. Place fabric pieces wrong sides together. Pin and stitch at a distance equal to half the seam allowance. Trim next to stitching.

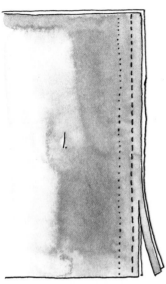

2. Fold fabrics right sides together. Pin and stitch along seamline. Press seam allowance to one side.

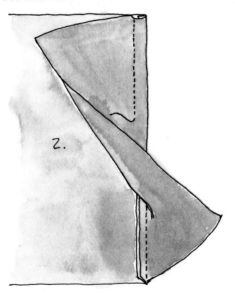

DOUBLE HEM

Turn up fabric edge twice, the same amount each time. Stitch hem. This gives a stable, opaque hem, useful for curtains.

TOPSTITCHING

Using a slightly longer stitch than usual and working from the right side of fabric, stitch parallel to the fabric edge. Heavy or contrasting coloured thread can be used for a more decorative effect.

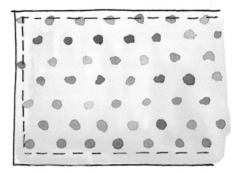

MARKING A LARGE CIRCLE

Fold fabric in half lengthways and then in half widthways. Tie one end of a string around a pencil and pin the other end to the fabric centre. Length of string should be half the desired diameter of the circle.

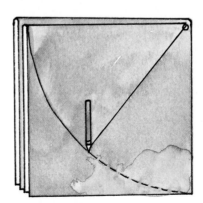

INDEX